The World At Home

You are holding a reproduction of an original work that is in the public domain in the United States of America, and possibly other countries. You may freely copy and distribute this work as no entity (individual or corporate) has a copyright on the body of the work. This book may contain prior copyright references, and library stamps (as most of these works were scanned from library copies). These have been scanned and retained as part of the historical artifact.

This book may have occasional imperfections such as missing or blurred pages, poor pictures, errant marks, etc. that were either part of the original artifact, or were introduced by the scanning process. We believe this work is culturally important, and despite the imperfections, have elected to bring it back into print as part of our continuing commitment to the preservation of printed works worldwide. We appreciate your understanding of the imperfections in the preservation process, and hope you enjoy this valuable book.

THE WORLD

AT HOME.

SCENE IN THE POLAR REGIONS.

T. Nelson and Sons, London, Edinburgh, and New York.

37.76
v3

THE WORLD

AT HOME;

OR,

PICTURES AND SCENES FROM FAR-OFF LANDS.

BY

Mary and Elizabeth Kirby,

AUTHORS OF "THINGS IN THE FOREST."

LONDON:
T. NELSON AND SONS, PATERNOSTER ROW;
EDINBURGH; AND NEW YORK.

1869.

[All Rights Reserved.]

Jur 269.6

v

Preface.

THIS volume is called "THE WORLD AT HOME," because it brings the world, that is so full of wonders, to our own fireside.

Young people can sit and read about the different races of men, the animals, the birds, the plants, and the insects, which they have never seen, and perhaps never heard of. As they read, they must admire the wisdom of the Creator in fitting every animal for the clime it has to live in, as well as in providing for its wants.

"The earth is the Lord's, and the fulness thereof." Hill and dale, flower and tree, sunrise and sunset, proclaim His power and His love.

The book is embellished with pictures of the various scenes and objects described, in order to make it more attractive.

It is intended to be followed by other volumes, which will carry the reader still further, and give him a taste for deeper research.

M. AND E. K.

Contents.

THE TOWER THAT WAS TO REACH THE SKY,	13
SOMETHING ABOUT THE WEATHER,	14
THE RED LIGHT IN THE SKY,	16
THE MAN DRAWN BY DOGS,	18
THE SEAL,	20
HOUSES MADE OF SNOW,	22
THE FIERCE WHITE BEAR,	24
THE WHALE,	25
THE GREENLANDER,	27
A FIGHT WITH THE WALRUS,	29
THE BUSY LITTLE LAPP,	33
SHIPS SET FAST IN THE ICE,	34
FLOCO AND HIS RAVENS,	38
THE WATER THAT SPOUTS AND BOILS,	41
MOUNT HECLA,	45
A LITTLE ABOUT ICELAND,	46
THE GULF STREAM,	48
THE POLAR SEA,	50
THE RED MAN,	51
THE BABY'S CRADLE,	54
THE MEDICINE-BAG,	56
THE FEAST OF GREEN CORN,	59
THE BUFFALO,	61
THE INDIAN WHEN HE IS OLD,	65
THE PRAIRIE ON FIRE,	66
THE HERONS IN THE CEDAR SWAMP,	70
SIR WALTER RALEIGH AND HIS TWO PLANTS,	73
THE WILD PIGEONS OF AMERICA,	75

CONTENTS.

THE BEAVER,	77
THE MAHOGANY TREE,	79
WHERE DOES THE COTTON COME FROM?	80
THE SUGAR-CANE,	84
WHERE DOES COCOA COME FROM?	88
THE FOREST IN BRAZIL,	92
THE INDIAN'S DRINKING FEAST,	95
THE TAPIR,	96
A LITTLE ABOUT BRAZIL,	100
THE INDIAN'S BOW AND ARROW,	103
THE MONKEY BRIDGE,	105
THE WARRIOR ANT,	106
THE ENEMY OF THE ANTS,	108
LEAVES WALKING,	110
THE HANGING NESTS,	111
INDIA-RUBBER,	113
THE EEL THAT GIVES A SHOCK,	114
A NARROW ESCAPE,	116
DIAMOND WASHING,	120
THE INDIAN'S MEDICINE,	121
THE GIANT TRUNKS,	125
THE INDIAN'S BLOW-PIPE,	126
THE GIANT WATER-LILY,	129
THE BABY'S BATH,	131
THE LAND OF THE GIANTS,	132
THE SAND STORM,	135
THE LIGHTS IN THE TREES,	137
THE CROCODILE IN THE MUD,	138
PAMPAS,	140
CROSSING THE ANDES,	142
THE HIGHEST VOLCANO IN THE WORLD,	144
THE COW TREE,	145
THE INDIAN'S BEAST OF BURDEN,	146
THE SHARK,	150
THE TYPHOON, OR GREAT WIND,	155
THE TEA-FARMER,	156
EATING BIRDS' NESTS,	160
THE CHINAMAN'S KNIFE AND FORK,	162
THE CHINAMAN'S DINNER,	163
FISHING WITH A BIRD,	164

CONTENTS.

TREPANG,	166
LITTLE FEET,	167
A CHINESE WEDDING,	168
RICE INSTEAD OF CORN,	169
BASKETS OF FIRE,	170
THE TALLOW TREE,	171
CHINAMAN BUSY IN A THICKET OF BAMBOO,	172
THE CITY ON THE WATERS,	175
A LITTLE ABOUT THE CHINAMAN'S RELIGION,	176
THE TWO EMPERORS,	177
THE BUTTERFLY TRICK,	179
SHOPPING IN JAPAN,	180
THE STEPPES,	184
BRICK TEA,	186
THE CAMEL OF THE TARTARS,	188
THE WILD HORSE OF THE STEPPES,	190
"THE SON OF HEAVEN,"	194
THE PRAYING-MILL,	195
THE TEMPLE OF GOLD,	196
A LITTLE MORE ABOUT THIBET,	198
THE YAK,	199
THE BUTTER FEAST,	200
THE PEARL DIVERS,	202
THE SPONGE AND THE CORAL,	204
THE MARK OF BUDDHA'S FOOT,	206
THE ELEPHANT,	208
THE TIGER HUNT,	210
THE TALIPOT,	212
THE HUMMING-BIRD,	213
THE SNAKE-CHARMER,	215
THE TURTLE,	217
THE BANIAN TREE,	220
THE GREAT SPIDER,	222
THE FLY-CATCHERS,	223
THE NUTMEG AND THE CLOVE,	226
THE BIRD OF PARADISE,	227
INSECTS THAT GIVE LIGHT,	229
THE HINDOO GOLDSMITH,	231
A LITTLE ABOUT CASTE,	233
GOING TO SCHOOL IN INDIA,	235

CONTENTS.

HOUSES IN INDIA,	238
THE SACRED RIVER,	239
BENARES,	242
THE MAN DROWNING HIMSELF IN THE RIVER GANGES,	244
THE BRAHMINS' KINDNESS TO DUMB ANIMALS,	246
THE TIGER OF THE JUNGLE,	247
THE BUNGALOW IN THE JUNGLE,	249
THINGS TO BE SEEN IN THE JUNGLE,	250
THE WET SEASON AND THE DRY,	254
BRIDGES IN INDIA,	256
THE STORY OF JUGGERNAUT,	257
THE GREAT BAT OF JAVA,	260
THE WILD MAN OF THE WOODS,	263
THE RAINLESS DESERT,	264
THE LION OF THE DESERT,	267
THE WIND OF THE DESERT,	268
THE SAND THAT LOOKS LIKE WATER,	272
MEN OF THE DESERT,	274
THE GREEN SPOT IN THE DESERT,	276
THE ARAB'S TENT,	278
FOOD OF THE ARABS,	280
ARABS AT DINNER,	283
COFFEE,	285
HOW DO THE ARABS DRESS?	289
THE ARAB'S LANCE,	291
WORKMEN IN THE DESERT,	293
THE GREAT BIRD OF THE DESERT,	294

THE WORLD AT HOME.

THE TOWER THAT WAS TO REACH THE SKY.

ONCE upon a time, the people who lived on the earth spoke the same language. But they became lifted up with pride. The earth had once been drowned by a flood. They thought, if they could build a tower high enough to reach to heaven, they never need fear a flood any more.

It was very wicked of them to think so. God had told them that He would never drown the world again; and they ought to have trusted His word.

And they might have known that no tower could be built by the hands of man which would be high enough to reach to heaven.

Did they build the tower?

They began to build it, but God stopped them.

He confounded their speech. That is, He made one man speak one language, and another man another language. So the men could not understand each other.

What a confusion there must have been! Of course, they could not go on building the tower. Each man went his own way, and the tower was given up.

Ever since that time different languages, or tongues, have been spoken all over the world. Each nation has its own language. In England, we speak English; and in France, people speak French; and so on.

But are the people who live in different parts of the world all alike? Oh no; far from it.

They have not the same colour, or the same features, or the same habits, or the same religion.

The happiest part of the world is where the Bible is read, and where the people are Christians. I think you will like to know something about other countries. You will find that people have a great many curious customs, and wear very curious dresses, and eat very curious things.

In some parts of the world it is very hot, in other parts very cold. In other places people are so happy as to live where it is neither hot nor cold.

But wherever men are placed, the good God provides them with enough to satisfy their wants. There is no part of the world where man can get out of the reach of God!

Are there any ruins of the tower?

There is a heap of bricks and rubbish, the remains of some great tower. The Arabs call it Babel.

The name they give it means confusion, or topsy-turvy.

SOMETHING ABOUT THE WEATHER.

THERE is a part of the world which is very hot indeed.

If you open the map of the world and spread it before you, I will tell you where it is.

Do you see a black line that runs through the middle of the map? That is called the Equator. There is no line in reality, but when ships pass through the place where the Equator is, they call it passing under the line.

The sailors have a great deal of fun when they pass under the line. Some of them dress up, and get into a boat, and then pretend to hail the ship.

One of the sailors is dressed up like Neptune, who was said, by the heathen, to be god of the sea. They give a little present to the captain, and dance on the deck and have very rough sports.

On each side of the Equator is the Torrid Zone. You can guess the meaning of the word *torrid*. It means very hot indeed. The sun is hotter than ever it is in England. Great palm-trees grow in the Torrid Zone, and large bright flowers, more beautiful than I can tell you. And there are wild beasts, and monkeys, and parrots, and humming-birds.

There is no winter at all. The leaves drop off the trees; but the new leaves have come before the old ones go. The trees are always green. It is summer all the year round.

How far does the Torrid Zone reach?

It reaches to two dotted lines that you can find, one on each side of the Equator.

Read their names.

The Tropic of Cancer to the north, and the Tropic of Capricorn to the south.

What kind of a climate do we come to, when we are out of the Torrid Zone?

To a climate where it is neither very hot nor very cold. Such a climate as England.

We are in the Temperate Zone. Here people can work hard, and not feel the worse for it. They can build great cities, and work with machines, and lead very active lives. The great nations of Europe are in the North Temperate Zone.

The South Temperate Zone has not many people in it. It is nearly all water.

Are there any more Zones?

Yes; there are the Frozen Zones. The countries round the North Pole are in the Frozen Zone. The South Frozen Zone has no countries in it that we know about. It is all sea and ice. The weather is very cold indeed in the Frozen Zone. The winter lasts nearly all the year round. The sea is blocked up with ice, and at last the ice and the cold will not let the sailors get any further.

THE FROZEN ZONE.

Do any people live in the Frozen Zone?

Yes; but they are scattered about over the country. They do not build houses. They keep shut up in huts a great part of the year. They have no fields of corn, and no machines to work with, and no books to read. No great nations are found in the Frozen Zone. It is too cold almost to live.

THE RED LIGHT IN THE SKY.

You never saw such a grand sight as this in your life! The sky is full of lights that keep dancing about, or else form a beautiful arch overhead.

THE RED LIGHT IN THE SKY, OR THE AURORA BOREALIS.

Your eyes would be almost dazzled by looking at them. Some of the lights are red, some are yellow, and some are purple. In fact, they are all the colours of the rainbow. It is the Frozen Zone where these lights shine the brightest. They seem as if they came to cheer up the poor people who live there.

In the winter, these poor people cannot see the sun for many weeks. I do not mean that the sky is clouded; but that the sun never shines above the horizon. Do you know what the horizon means?

You must go up a hill, and then look round. You will see, in the distance, that there is a line where the sky seems to touch the ground. That line is the horizon. If it is very early in the morning, you may perhaps see a rosy light in the east. And then up will come the golden ball of the sun. But in the Frozen Zone, if it was winter, you might watch all day and not see the sun. The stars would keep on shining as if it was night.

About noon there would be a faint kind of glimmer like what twilight is in England. But the sun would never show his face at all.

While the sun is away, the stars shine brighter than ever they do anywhere else. And the beautiful lights will come and dance in the sky. The people can see to go about, or even to work, by the shining of these lights. They would be very badly off without them.

What is the name of the lights?

Aurora Borealis; or, what is a prettier name still, "the merry dancers."

THE MAN DRAWN BY DOGS.

HERE are some of the people who live in the Frozen Zone. They are called Esquimaux. They do not grow very tall, because of the cold. But they know how to wrap themselves up in furs and skins. They would be frozen to death if they did not. Where do the furs and skins come from? God has made some animals to live in the Frozen Zone which are of use to the Esquimaux.

The bear gives him his nice warm fur, or rather the Esquimaux takes it from him.

And there is a funny creature that lives in the sea, and has a round head and a tail like a fish. This is the seal; and its skin is as warm as anything he can find. So he makes his coat, and his cap, and his shoes of it.

But no animal is more useful to the Esquimaux than his dog. His dog stands to him in the place of a horse. There are no horses in this country. They could not live. There is nothing for them to eat, and there are no roads for them to gallop on.

So when he wants to go a journey he has to be drawn by dogs. The carriage he rides in is a sledge. He made it himself out of the bones of the great whale. Then he covered it with seal-skin. You can see the shape of the sledge as well as if it was standing before you. The poor dogs have very long journeys to go. You see how they are fastened together with straps of seal-skin. The dog that runs first is called a leader, and the driver tells him which way to go.

If the man says "Nannook," the dogs will run as fast again as they did before.

Nannook is the name, in that country, of the fierce white bear. The dogs go hunting with their master, and help to get him his food. They hate the white bear, and like nothing so much as running him down.

Their master knows this, and he often plays them a trick. He will cry out "Nannook!" when no bear is in sight. He only wants the dogs to go a little quicker.

The leader is a very clever dog, and does not often make a mistake.

THE MAN DRAWN BY DOGS.

If there is a snow-drift, or if the night is dark, he will put his nose to the ground, and run along straight to the place where he is going.

The driver is not very kind to his dogs. In the winter he gives them very little to eat. One reason is that he gets very little for himself. But his wife feeds them whenever she can; and when they are ill, she lets them lie down in the hut, and takes care of them. The dogs are very fond of their mistress, and will follow her anywhere. If they are ever so hungry, they will come out when she calls them, and be harnessed to the sledge.

But one thing the poor dogs cannot help doing. If they see a morsel of anything to eat lying by the side of the road, they will run to it. In vain the driver scolds and beats them. They will not stir until they have eaten it up.

Of course the dogs steal as much as they can of their master's food. Then the Esquimaux is very angry indeed. Half his time is spent in driving the dogs out of the hut, and watching lest they should steal his dinner.

How much better it would be, if he let the poor dogs have some dinner as well!

THE SEAL.

The poor Esquimaux takes a great deal of trouble to catch the seal.

The seal is very cunning, and does not mean to be caught if he can help it.

He loves to swim about all day in the water. But he will sometimes take a nap on the ice.

He is so cautious that he will seem to sleep with his eyes open.

He will dive into the sea at the least noise. Not that he is quick.

He is very fat and very slow. But he takes care to be near a hole in the ice, so that he can pop down in a minute.

Many of the holes in the ice have been made by the seal himself.

He makes them, that he may put up his round head and breathe.

The Esquimaux goes about and listens. He is trying to hear a seal

THE SEAL. 21

THE SEAL.

making a hole. If he hears the seal breathe, he will not leave the spot—no, let the cold be ever so great!

He wants to get that seal, and take it home to his wife and children.

He makes a little wall of snow to keep the wind off him. And then he squats down and waits.

Meanwhile, the seal goes on working. It does not know that its enemy is lying in wait.

It goes on till the ice gets very thin indeed, and the hole nearly broken through.

But it takes a long time to make the hole. And the poor Esquimaux is sitting all the time in the cold. His spear lies at his side, ready to be used when it is wanted.

If he stirred or made the slightest noise, the seal would hear him and go away.

The funniest thing is, that he will tie his own knees together for fear his clothes should make a rustling.

All at once the right moment is come. He lifts up his spear without making any sound, and drives it with all his might into the seal's body.

He has a rope round his arm, and he ties it to the seal and drags it out.

When the seal is fairly caught and killed, there is a great rejoicing.

The women and children come out of the huts to meet the hunter, and to tell him how glad they are.

They have perhaps been without meat for some time. And they have had no oil in their lamps. They could not even melt the snow into water when they wanted something to drink.

But now a time of plenty begins. The lamps swim with oil. The women bring out their cooking-pots, and get the feast ready.

Children snatch up bits of raw seal, and put them into their mouths, and suck them as if they were pieces of sugar-candy.

HOUSES MADE OF SNOW.

THERE are no nice houses or towns in the Frozen Zone. The Esquimaux do not know how to build them. All the winter they live in huts made of snow.

The snow hut is very clean and white when it is new. But it soon gets dirty. And when the summer comes it begins to melt.

The Esquimaux does not always make his hut of snow. Sometimes he finds logs of wood on the shore. They have not grown in his own country. No trees grow there. But they have been drifted by the waves from some other place; and then he picks them up and builds his hut with them.

When he cannot get wood, he uses the pure white snow.

HOUSES MADE OF SNOW.

MAKING SNOW HOUSES.

It is so hard frozen that it will not melt. It keeps hard all through the winter. Sometimes, when the hut gets very warm with the lamps and the people and the dogs, the walls begin to drip a little. But he takes a piece of fresh snow, and soon mends the place.

Has he windows to his house?

Yes; but they are not made of glass. No one can make glass in this country. The window is a piece of ice.

Is not the snow very cold?

Oh no! the hut is as warm as the Esquimaux can bear it. He has no fire either.

How does he warm it, then?

By his lamp. His lamp is nothing but a vessel like a saucer, which is full of oil. A great many little wicks float on the oil, and he lights them all. The burning wicks make the room warm.

A cooking pot hangs over the lamp; but he often likes to eat his meat raw. Has he any chairs or tables?

Oh no! People do not know how to make them. There is a seat all round the hut. It is covered with warm skins, and does to sit or to lie upon. But if you took a peep under the skins, you would see that the seat was of snow.

When the warm weather comes the Esquimaux is glad to get away from the snow hut. Its walls begin to drip, and he gets wet as he lies in bed. He often takes cold if he cannot go at once and live in a tent.

He lives in a tent all the summer.

THE FIERCE WHITE BEAR.

THE fierce white bear lives in the sea as much as on the land. He lives in the cold country where the man was drawn about by dogs. He is called the "ice bear," because he keeps so much on the ice. His fur is white and sleek, and his toes are joined together, very much like the toes of a duck or a goose. He can swim as well as a fish can, and is as much at home in the water.

When he gets on land, he can run a great deal faster than a man can. Indeed, a man would never get away from him by running.

THE FIERCE WHITE BEAR.

The white bear eats fish, and birds, and foxes, and even the reindeer when he can get it.

He is very savage when he is hungry. In the picture he has caught a seal. The seal was lying on the ice taking a nap, when the fierce bear came stealing along. His feet made no noise, and the poor seal did not awake in time. When he did awake it was too late. The fierce bear will eat him up every bit.

I am glad there are no fierce white bears in England!

THE WHALE.

PEOPLE meet with a great many hardships when they go to hunt the great whale.

The whale is the biggest creature that man knows anything about.

No animal, on sea or land, is so large as the whale.

Is not the whale a fish?

No; it is an animal, though it looks like a fish, and many people call it one.

It has warm red blood, and the fish has cold blood. It gives suck to its young, and it cannot live except it breathes air.

It has two holes in the top part of the head, called blow-holes.

It will blow out a great stream or jet of something that looks like water.

But the jet is not really water. It is a steam or vapour. The breath, in fact, of the whale. When the warm vapour comes into the cold air, it turns to a cloud of mist, and falls like water. The whales are very fond of blowing.

They make such a great noise when they are angry that it may be heard for miles off.

The mother whale is very fond of her little one. She will come swimming up in a moment if she thinks it is in danger.

The men who are in the ship looking out for the whale know this. If they see a little whale, they will fling a harpoon and try to wound it. They know this will bring out the mother, as fast as she can get.

THE WHALE.

KILLING THE GREAT WHALE.

They want to kill the mother whale, for the sake of the oil in her body.

They get into a boat, as you see in the picture, and begin to throw their harpoons. A very long rope is fastened to the harpoon, and the other end of the rope is in the boat.

The sailors have a machine like a wheel, on which the rope is wound. It is called a windlass. The windlass turns round very quickly indeed, when the harpoon is lodged in the body of the whale. For the whale dives down to the bottom of the sea, carrying the harpoon with it.

If a sailor gets his feet entangled in the rope, he would not be able to get them free, while it was being pulled by the whale. And he would very likely be dragged overboard and drowned.

Indeed, from first to last, there is great danger in hunting the whale.

Sometimes the whale will give the boat such a blow with its tail that it is thrown up into the air, and all the sailors with it.

The sailors are very much afraid of the huge tail of the whale, and get as far from it as they can.

The whale cannot keep at the bottom of the sea long, because it must come up to breathe. It takes care to come up a long way from the boat. But the sailors can always tell where it has gone to. The harpoon is still in its body, and the rope fast to it. So they pull at the oars, and soon come up with the poor whale.

The whale dives again, when it feels another harpoon. But it cannot help coming up, as it did before. And so the hunt goes on till the whale is tired out and weak from loss of blood. Then the sailors can come quite close up and kill it.

What people live in that country?

The Greenlanders. They are like the Esquimaux, and think the whale a great treat.

There are many kinds of whales, and they are found in different places in the world.

The whale in the picture is the great Greenland whale.

What does the whale eat?

It eats tiny shell-fish and little soft-bodied creatures called jelly-fish

It swims with its great mouth wide open. A fringe of hairs hangs down from the roof of its mouth.

Its mouth is like a cavern, for it is nearly half as large as its body.

All the little creatures it wants to swallow abound everywhere in the sea, and they swim into its mouth by thousands. But they cannot get out again. The fringe prevents that. They are gulped down by the whale. It takes many such mouthfuls to make the huge creature a dinner.

THE GREENLANDER.

THE man in the picture is a Greenlander, and he is going out in his boat.

Summer is come, and he wants to hunt for the walrus or the narwhal.

What is the narwhal?

THE GREENLANDER.

THE GREENLANDER IN HIS BOAT.

A kind of whale, with a long spike to its upper lip.

He has made the boat himself. He made it of whalebone, and then covered it with the skin of the seal. The seal-skin fits tight round his waist, and will not let in a drop of water. He can never get wet in his water-tight boat. If the weather is ever so stormy, he does not mind. If a great wave knocks him over, he can soon right himself with his paddle.

He has the paddle in his hand. It is like an oar, only wide at both ends.

The Greenlander has a house made of great stones. He contrives to roof it with pieces of wood that are thrown on shore by the sea. He is very careful of his wood, and never makes a fire of it. He warms his house with a lamp as the Esquimaux does.

Several families live in one house. There are partitions made to keep them separate. The houses have windows, but very little air is let in. You creep into the house through a dark narrow passage.

The Greenlander catches the seal as the Esquimaux does. The flesh of the seal is being cooked all day long. If a visitor comes in, he is asked to eat some.

No corn grows in Greenland, and the reindeer runs wild. So there is no reindeer's milk to be had.

The Greenlander hunts the reindeer, and kills it when he can for the sake of its flesh.

You would think a Greenlander would like to live in England. He would have the sun shining all the year round, and he would live in a good house, and have plenty of food without hunting for it.

But he does not like to live in England. Some Greenlanders came here once, and people wanted them to stay. But they began to fret and pine. They liked their own country the best.

A FIGHT WITH THE WALRUS.

A GREAT many huge creatures live in the Frozen Zone. There is the whale. His body looks almost like an island. And there is the walrus.

In the picture the walruses look very fierce indeed; but they are angry. They were lying on shore asleep, and the men came and tried to kill them. Then they got up, and tumbled one over the other into the sea. They made such haste, and were so big, that the men could not stop them. But when they had all tumbled into the sea, the men put off in a boat, and rowed after them. Then you see what took place. The walruses were still very angry; and they felt braver in the sea than they did on the land. So they got round the boat and tried to upset it. The men will have hard work to drive them away, or to kill them.

A FIGHT WITH THE WALRUS.

A FIGHT WITH THE WALRUS.

Why do the men want to kill the walrus?

Because his great body is so useful to them.

Do you see his long tusks? They are white and shining, and are made of ivory. He has a thick, tough skin, and it can be made into good leather. His flesh is a great feast to the people on shore, though you and I might not like it.

Though the walrus is so big, and has such fierce-looking tusks, he does no harm. He has no front teeth, and could not eat flesh if he tried. He eats sea-weed and little shell-fishes that he finds in the sea.

His tusks are very useful to him when he is on the ice. He can stick them into a great rock of ice and drag himself up.

When the fierce white bear attacks him, he fights with his tusks. It will be well for the sailors in the boat if he does not make them feel his tusks as well.

THE REINDEER BEING MILKED.

THE BUSY LITTLE LAPP.

THERE is a tribe of busy little people who live in the Frozen Zone, and are very seldom seen anywhere else. They do not live in huts, because it would not suit them to do so. They are obliged to wander up and down the country. Sometimes they are in the mountains, and sometimes in the plains. So they pitch tents, and then they can move about as they like.

They are called Lapps, which is short for Laplander. Lapland is the name of the country where they live. You can find it by looking on the map of Europe. The reason why the Lapp moves about so much, is because of a very useful animal that God has given him.

I mean the reindeer. The reindeer likes to move about. In the summer some very fierce flies bite him. The flies are called mosquitoes. I am happy to say we have not any in England. When the mosquitoes bite him, the poor deer is glad to run anywhere. He runs up the cold mountains, and likes to stay there. Then the Lapp follows him, and sets up his tent.

In the winter, the flies go away, and then the Lapp drives his reindeer down to the plain. So you see he has to set up his tent again. You would not think the tent very nice to live in. The door is so small you can hardly get in. There is no chimney, but the smoke goes out at a hole in the top,—that is, it goes out after it has made everybody's face look very black.

There are no lamps or candles. People think the fire-light is enough. They sit and they sleep on skins spread on the floor. They find out the time by looking at the sun. How many things the little Lapp has to do without!

But he is very happy and contented. If he has a herd of reindeer, he thinks he is a rich man. He has very little to eat besides the flesh and the milk of the reindeer. When winter comes, and the wild-fowl have flown away, and the sea is too frozen to let him catch fish, he goes to his herd of reindeer and kills one of them.

This is as good to him as beef or mutton is to us.

Every morning and night the reindeer are fetched up to be milked.

The milk they give is thicker and nicer than that of the cow. The Lapp wife makes cheese of it. She does not use butter.

There is a man in the picture who is riding on a sledge. He has no horse to draw him. But see how his reindeer gallops away! The reindeer is fastened to the sledge by a strap, and his master ties a cord round his horns by way of a bridle. His master can go a great many miles drawn by his faithful reindeer.

When the reindeer dies, or is killed, his warm skin makes a coat or rug, or whatever garment the Lapp chooses to have.

So that the reindeer may be said to feed and to clothe his master.

What does the reindeer live upon? Nothing except moss. This moss grows under the snow, and seems to have been put there on purpose for the reindeer. In winter, when it freezes so hard that you could not stand out in it a minute, the reindeer wanders about looking for moss. He has no stable or shelter of any kind. But he turns up the frozen snow, and gets at the moss, and is quite content. A horse or a cow would die if turned out in such a frost. But this is the home of the reindeer. He will not die, for God has placed him there to be a comfort to the little Lapp.

SHIPS SET FAST IN THE ICE.

PEOPLE in England are very fond of finding things out. They have found out how to make steam work like a horse. And they have found out how to send messages by the wires that run along the side of the railway.

But there was another thing people wanted to find out. They wanted to find out what they call "The North-West Passage." I will try to explain to you what the North-West Passage is.

If you look at the map of the world you will see two great pieces of water. One is called the Atlantic and the other the Pacific Ocean. Now, to get from the Atlantic to the Pacific, ships have to go round South America by Cape Horn, or else round Africa by the Cape of Good Hope.

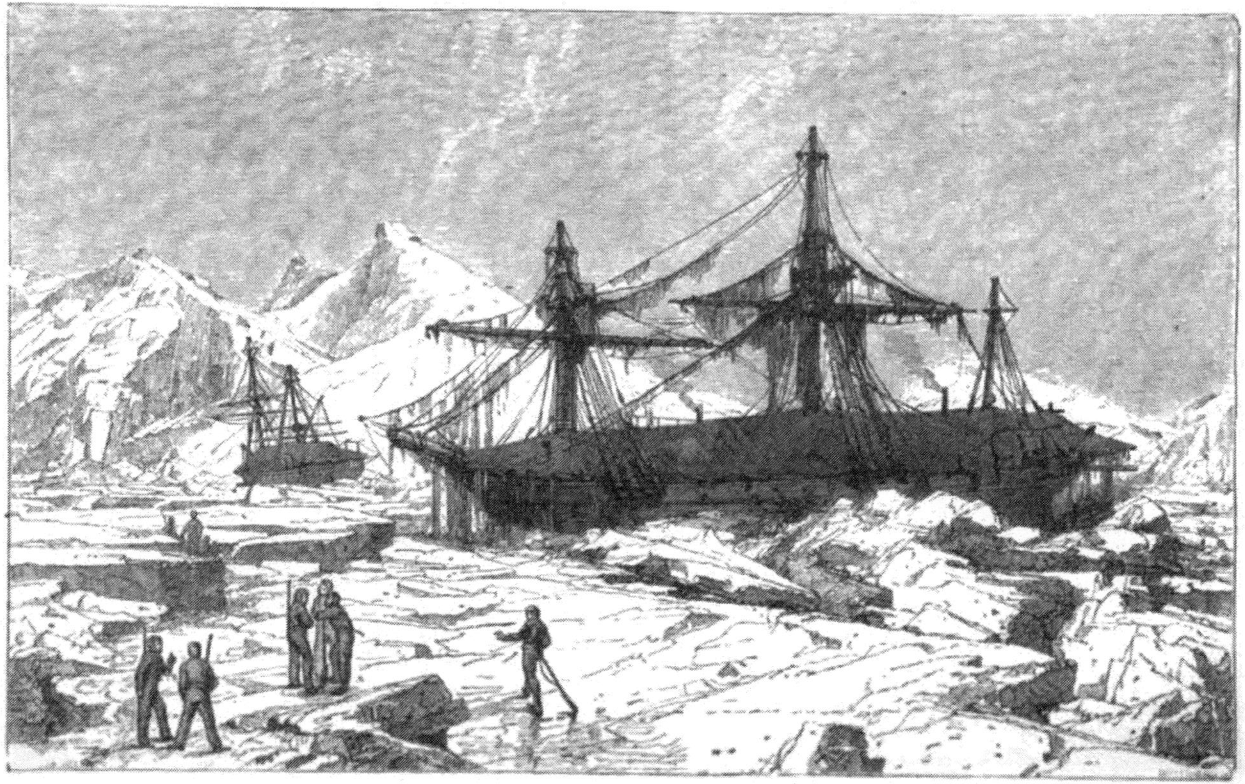

FAST IN THE ICE

SHIPS SET FAST IN THE ICE.

It was thought that a way might be made for ships to sail along the extreme north coast of America and come out into the Pacific Ocean.

This was called "The North-West Passage." It would be a short route, and would save a great many miles.

First one brave man and then another has been to try. They found out a great many straits and bays. And they named them after themselves. There is "Baffin's Bay," and "Hudson's Bay," and "Davis' Straits."

But the brave men always met with an enemy that made them turn back. I mean the cold.

It is the Frozen Zone, and the sea is frozen over. If the ice melts a little in the summer, there are still great dangers. Huge blocks of ice are floating about; and if they were to come against the ship, they would knock it all to pieces. These blocks of ice are as large as mountains, and very grand to look at. They are green and blue, and a great many colours, and they shine as clear and bright as crystal. But the sailors try to keep out of their way.

Perhaps you have heard the name of Captain Franklin. He was a very brave man indeed, and had set his mind on finding out the North-West Passage. He tried again and again; and the last time he went to try he never came back any more.

If you look at the picture you will see what happened to him. His ships were set fast in the ice. He knew this was likely to happen, and had brought plenty of food.

He did all he could to take care of his men. He made them run about to keep themselves warm. If the weather was very bad they would run about the deck. And sometimes the men would sing by way of cheering each other's spirits. There they are upon the ice. I daresay those three are talking about dear Old England.

It is very cold; so cold that you could hardly bear it. The men had often to cover their faces with a veil or mask to keep them from being frost-bitten.

Poor Captain Franklin had to leave his ships at last. The ice did not melt, and there was no hope of getting through it. Besides, the food was being used up. All the animals, except the wolves and the foxes, were gone to a warmer place; and there was no fishing in the ice. When the ship is left, the only way is, for the sailors to draw the boats along upon the ice until they get to a place where the sea is not frozen. And this is what they tried to do.

Captain Franklin did not come back to England; and then a ship was sent out to look for him. This ship was called the *Fox*, and I am sorry to tell you the news it brought.

Poor Captain Franklin had died in that dreadful country, and most of his men had died too.

The captain of the *Fox* did not meet with a single man belonging to the crew. But he saw many things that made him sad. In one place there was a boat that the poor sailors had been trying to drag along. Near the boat, there lay scattered about on the ice a pair of worked slippers, and a watch, and a Bible. I am glad to tell you that the Bible seemed to have been a comfort to its owner. There were marks and bits of writing in it in pencil, as if it had been read and thought about a great deal.

Thanks to all the searching, and the brave captains who have gone in ships to look for it, the North-West Passage has been found out. But while the ice and snow remain as they are, no ships will be able to make use of it.

Another way has been thought of—a canal to go through that narrow strip of land that joins North and South America together. Should that canal ever be made, a ship will then be able to sail through it from the Atlantic and come out into the Pacific Ocean.

FLOCO AND HIS RAVENS.

Do you know what is meant by a pirate?

A pirate is a man who goes out to sea in a vessel and tries to rob all the other vessels that he meets with.

FLOCO AND HIS RAVENS.

Once there used to be a great many pirates sailing about in the seas of Europe. It is a good thing that there are very few in these days.

The ships in which these pirates sailed were not like the ships of our day. Here is a picture of one of them.

The bow was formed like a huge dragon, which seemed to cut the waves with its gaudily-painted breast.

Its tail curled behind, over the head of the steersman.

Twenty or thirty long oars were used on each side. A single mast bore a large square sail, made in broad stripes of red, white, and blue.

ANCIENT SHIP.

Well were these pirate ships known on the shores of Britain.

A great many years ago, one of these pirates was caught in a dreadful storm. His ship had to run before the wind—that is, he had no power to guide it. The ship went wherever the wind chose to drive it.

Where did the ship drive to?

To an island nearly covered with snow. There were no people on this island; but he saw mountains with peaks white with snow. There was so much snow that he called it Snowland.

When he got home to Norway, he told his friends he had found a new island; and he talked so much about it, that another man went out in a ship to look what kind of a place Snowland really was.

The mariner's compass was not invented in those days. Do you know what the mariner's compass is like?

It is a box with a needle fastened in it. The needle can turn round any way; but it always points to the north. When the sailor is wandering in his vessel over the wide ocean, and there are no stars to guide him, he looks at his compass. Then he can always tell which is the north, and which way to go.

The man who went to look for Snowland was called Floco. He took three ravens with him. He thought that when he had sailed a good way on he would let one of them fly. He hoped it would fly to land, and then he would sail after it.

But the first raven he let go did not fly forward. It went back to the place from which it had been brought. Then Floco knew that he had not sailed far enough. He was nearer to his own country than he was to Snowland.

A few days after he let the second raven loose. But the raven, after flying about a long time as if it did not know where to go, came back to the ship.

No land was to be seen.

At last Floco let loose the third raven. This time he was right. The bird flew straight to land.

Floco was very glad indeed to think that he was so near the end of his voyage.

Soon he came in sight of the island of Snowland; but there was so much ice all about it that he changed its name, and called it Iceland.

He stayed about a year in Iceland, and then went home.

A very cruel king reigned in Norway in those days, and many of the rich nobles wanted to get out of his way.

They had heard a great deal about Iceland, and they thought they could not do better than go there. After talking about it a long time, two of them set sail with their wives and children.

They found the whole island covered with trees; and that nobody lived there.

They had to chop the trees down as they pushed their way along.

A great many more people came from Norway to escape the cruel king. So that Iceland was inhabited.

What religion had the people of Iceland in those days?

. They were heathens. They made sacrifices to their gods. Often human beings were offered upon the altars. But missionaries soon began to come to Iceland to teach the people better.

At first the poor ignorant heathen pelted these good men with stones, and would not listen to them. But the missionaries kept on coming, and by degrees the Icelanders began to listen to them.

At length the people met together to talk the matter over. They made up their minds to throw their idols away, and not worship them any more.

Who did they worship?

The true God, and our Saviour Jesus Christ.

Does Iceland now belong to Norway?

No; it belongs to Denmark.

Should you like to know the name of the cruel king who drove the nobles away?

It was Harold Harfager. And the first two nobles went out in the year A.D. 874.

THE WATER THAT SPOUTS AND BOILS.

Is Iceland in the Frozen Zone?

No; but it lies very close to it.

It is in the North Temperate Zone. But it is much colder than in England. England lies further from the Frozen Zone than Iceland does.

Iceland is all over hills and rocks; and sometimes the ground is strewed with stones and pieces of a black burnt substance called lava.

Where does the lava come from?

From some mountains called volcanoes. Once the lava was thrown out burning hot from a hole at the top. It ran down the sides of the mountains; and looked like melted stones.

That was a very long time ago. All the volcanoes have given over sending up stones except one.

THE WATER THAT SPOUTS AND BOILS.

THE GREAT GEYSER.

That one is Mount Hecla, and it has not thrown up any stones lately.

But though the volcanoes seem to be quiet, they are working away underground. Though there is ice at the top of the ground, there is fire beneath.

The fire goes working on a long way. When it meets with water it makes it boil. If you listen in some places, and put your ear close to the ground, you can hear the hissing of steam and a rumbling noise a little like thunder.

Fire and water are meeting each other. When the water finds a place where it can get out it spouts up like a fountain. It is so hot that you could boil your kettle over it. It keeps on spouting in the same place till it has worn itself a smooth basin. All round the basin are the stones it has thrown up.

When it has spouted a few minutes it goes down into the basin. But it soon comes up again, and spouts as fiercely as ever.

Travellers always go to see the hot springs. Indeed, some people travel to Iceland on purpose. There are a number of them to see. There is the big Geyser and the little Geyser, and others besides.

Geyser is a good name for them. It means to spout or rage.

MOUNT HECLA

MOUNT HECLA.

One day a shower of ashes fell on some islands near the coast of Scotland, called the Orkney Islands.

This happened rather more than twenty years ago.

People knew that the ashes came from a volcano; and they guessed that Mount Hecla was throwing them out.

This was indeed the truth. News very soon came of what was going on in Iceland. An earthquake had happened in the night, and loud noises had been heard, like something roaring under-ground.

The people were very much frightened, as you may think. But the next day they were more frightened still. There came a loud crash, and Mount Hecla began to throw out fire and smoke.

The fire ran down the sides of the mountain, and burnt up everything it met.

Some poor sheep were feeding on a common. Those which could not get away quick enough were killed.

The mountain was dreadful to look at. It was wrapped in clouds of steam and ashes. The rivers, near where the lava flowed, grew so hot that all the fishes died.

A fortnight after, there came another crash. Everybody in the island could hear it; and the lava burst out afresh, and ran for more than twenty miles!

It was like a stream of fire, and was a mile broad. All the ice and snow on the mountain melted, and made a great flood.

You may think what harm was done to the country.

Even where a bit of grass was left, it was quite spoiled. It seemed as if it had been poisoned. And if the cattle ate any of it, they were taken ill, and died.

All the while the mountain was throwing out lava, there was a great storm of thunder and lightning. And often the red light would shine in the sky.

Some of the stones thrown out were immensely large, and were carried to a distance of five miles.

A LITTLE ABOUT ICELAND.

There is only one town in all Iceland, and that is by the sea-side. It is a very poor place, not much better than a village.

The people live by the sea-side in order to catch the fish. They have wooden houses, with painted doors to make them look smart.

There are no inns. An inn-keeper would not find much custom in Iceland.

When a man wants an inn he goes to the church.

The church is used for many purposes besides preaching in.

A gentleman once went to church in Iceland. He saw the people sitting on great boxes instead of in pews. He asked the reason why, and was told,—

"Oh, sir, we keep our best clothes in the boxes!"

There was no lock on the church-door, and a man could go in and out to his box, just as he liked.

How curious that would be thought in England!

The farmer keeps his bags in the church, and makes it quite a lumber room. People have to eat and sleep in it, when they use it for an inn.

The churches are a long way off each other. There are not many of them in Iceland.

What kind of houses are those little wooden ones, inside?

They look smart enough with their green shutters; but they are not very comfortable. The windows are very small, and are not opened enough. The Icelanders are not fond of fresh air, or of pure water.

They are very dirty people, and wash neither themselves nor their clothes half as often as they should do. They ride on brisk little horses, that trot up and down the rough places, and do not often stumble. And they catch a great deal of fish in summer, and salt it for the winter. They eat fish and butter. The butter is squeezed very dry and packed up to keep a long time. We should think it rancid stuff.

The rich people eat beef, and mutton, and rye bread. No corn can grow in Iceland. And some of the rich people have larger houses and better built. The doors and windows, and most of the fittings, are brought over from Denmark.

How do the people of Iceland dress?

They wear woollen clothes to keep themselves warm. The rich women are very smart indeed. An Iceland lady will have on a blue cloth petticoat, and a scarlet boddice, and a ruff of red and blue round her neck. She will have silver chains in her hair, and put on a curious high head-dress with a handkerchief at the top.

The wool comes from the sheep. But there are no machines in Iceland to make it into cloth. The women wash it and spin it themselves.

They are very busy in the long winter evenings. For they make the cloth into petticoats, and knit their own gloves and stockings.

Besides all this, they get the eider down ready for sale.

EIDER DUCKS.

The eider down is very soft and warm. It comes from the breast of a duck, and is used to make quilts of.

If you were to kill an eider duck people would be very angry.

There is one place where the nests are so close together that you can hardly help treading upon them. And the birds are so tame they will not move out of your way.

The duck pulls the soft down off her breast to line the nest with, and make a bed for her young ducklings.

But the Icelander comes creeping up when the duck is not at home, and takes away the down.

He takes an egg or two as well. For he thinks the eggs very nice to eat.

When the duck comes back and finds the down gone, she sets to work and pulls some more off.

Her breast soon loses all its down, and then her mate pulls off some of his.

The ducks do not stay all the year in Iceland. When the little ones can swim they all go off, and not one of them is to be seen.

But the Iceland woman has a great quantity of down that has been stolen from the nests. She mixes it with feathers and straw to make it go further. And when it is all ready, she sells it to make into quilts and petticoats.

THE GULF STREAM.

ONCE upon a time, people did not know that there was such a place as America.

But some clever men, who thought a great deal, wondered where certain things came from.

Some trees were cast up on the shore, and these trees did not grow anywhere either in Europe, or Asia, or Africa.

Where could they have drifted from?

We know where they had drifted from. They had drifted on the sea all the way from America.

A stream or current of water brought them. It is called the Gulf Stream.

This stream is warmer than the rest of the sea, and is of a different colour. It comes from the Torrid Zone, and flows on through the sea for a very long way.

Why is it called the Gulf Stream?

Because it has travelled round the Gulf of Mexico. When it comes out, people name it the Gulf Stream. The Gulf Stream does England a great deal of good. Without it the weather would be very cold indeed. Our seas would be blocked up with ice, and our ships could not sail about for a great part of the year.

We might as well live in the Frozen Zone as in England without the Gulf Stream.

But the stream of warm water comes straight from the Gulf of Mexico to the western shores of Europe. It makes the climate mild, and prevents the sea from ever being blocked up with ice.

THE GRAPE WEED.

There are some parts of America quite as far from the Frozen Zone as England is. But they are as cold as Iceland, or the country where the poor Esquimaux live. The reason is, because the Gulf Stream does not flow that way to warm them.

Fishes and animals that live in the seas of the Torrid Zone are sometimes carried along in the Gulf Stream as far as the British shores. They have kept in the stream all the way, or the cold of our seas would have killed them.

There is a curious sea-weed that floats in the Gulf Stream. It has seeds upon it that look like little bunches of grapes. The sailors call it the grape-weed, and they are very fond of bringing some home in a bottle to show to their friends. There is such a great deal of this weed, in one place, that ships are almost set fast in it.

How thankful we ought to be that the Gulf Stream flows near enough to give us some of its warmth, and that we are not frozen up like the poor Esquimaux!

THE POLAR SEA.

Is there a sea of water round the North Pole? I thought it was all ice.

And so many people thought; and many brave men have been turned back by the cold.

But in these days, something new is always being found out.

A clever man, named Dr. Kane, stayed all the winter up in the ice. When the spring came, he got his ship along, and still kept going towards the Pole.

He went on for more than a hundred miles, and then the ice actually came to an end! An open sea, like that in the picture, rolled at his feet. The water was of a green colour, and felt almost warm. The waves were dashing, and wild-fowl and sea-gulls were flying about and enjoying themselves. The air felt milder, instead of colder, and he could hardly believe he was so near the North Pole.

You may think how glad he was! And what wonderful news he had to bring home with him! In the picture, one of the men is setting up a flag, as a sign of victory.

It is an American flag, because the captain of the ship was an American.

Did he go any further?

No. The sailors were so worn out with the hardships they had gone through, they could go no further.

When they had planted their flag, and enjoyed the sight of the polar sea, they turned back. But more people are gone, and we hope soon to know all about it.

THE POLAR SEA.

I have just told you how the Gulf Stream makes England warm. It is thought that a current of the same warm water flows to the Pole, and may be the reason of the open sea.

THE RED MAN.

Who lived in America when the white man came there?

A great many people lived there. They had not white skins as we have. Their skins were a reddish-brown, or copper coloured. They were called Indians. We call them American Indians.

It was a glorious country for any one to live in. There were rivers full of fish, and forests full of game. And there were buffaloes, and wild horses, and deer and turkeys, and pigeons without number.

But, in spite of this, the white man is driving the red man quite out of the country.

The reason is, the white man gets all kinds of knowledge. He has learned to make ships and guns, and machines of every sort you can think of. He is always learning and making something new.

The red man does not care to learn. He knows how to hunt and to fish. He can find his way through the deep forests. He can tell you the track of the wild animal by the slightest mark on the ground. He knows a great deal about the use of the plants and herbs that grow in the forest.

But when he has killed enough game to satisfy his hunger, and when he has made a roof of some kind to shelter him, he is content. He does not want to be troubled with knowledge or improvements. So when the white man begins to clear the forest, and to build houses, and to grow corn, the red man retires from before him. He goes away to some place where he can do as he likes, and not be disturbed. So the white man gets stronger, and the red man weaker.

I must tell you something about the red man.

He is very tall and fine looking. He would be handsome, if he did not paint his face as you see in the picture.

He wears a strip of soft leather wrapped round his foot instead of a shoe. He calls it a mocassin. His stockings or leggings are of cloth or leather, and are stitched on, and not taken off. He does not wear his best clothes every day. He paints his body, and wears a short kind of skirt, with a girdle round his waist, and a plume of feathers on his head. But when he wants to be grand, he puts on his robes.

His robe is of skin, taken from the buffalo or the deer. But it is very much adorned with figures, and with porcupines' quills. And often it has a deep fringe upon it.

What is the fringe made of?

I am sorry to tell you that it is made of human hair. The hair of the men he has killed, because they were his enemies.

It is one of his customs to scalp his enemy when he has killed him.

THE RED MAN.

THE RED MAN.

Then he flourishes the scalp in his hands, holding it by the hair. The more scalps he can get, the better he is thought of.

From this you perceive that the red man is not a Christian.

He worships a being whom he calls the Great Spirit. He prays to him, and calls him Father.

But the Indian has no Bible, and no knowledge of Jesus Christ.

He thinks there is an Evil Spirit who can get the mastery over the Good Spirit. What a sad idea that is! The Indian is always afraid lest the Evil Spirit should do him harm. When he is ill, and feels as if he were going to die, he sends for the medicine-man.

Is the medicine-man a doctor?

Yes, he is a doctor, though that is not all. He can prescribe medicine, which he makes out of the herbs that grow in the forest. And sometimes the medicine does the patient good. Whether it does him good or not he must take it, for there is no other doctor to be had.

What else does the medicine-man do?

He is the *mystery* man. That is, he pretends to have power over the Evil Spirit. And this is why the Indian sends for him, when he thinks he is going to die.

He comes dressed up in the skin of some wild animal, so that you might almost fancy it was the animal itself walking in. He makes a dreadful noise, and shakes his spear, and dances, and rattles bones together, and grunts, and howls. He would be turned out, in a moment, if the tent belonged to the white man. But the poor Indians stand by in silence, and look on with awe. They think all the noise and howling will drive away the Evil Spirit.

If the poor patient dies in the midst of the tumult, the medicine-man says it is the will of the Great Spirit. And he packs up his traps and goes off. Perhaps to dance and howl by the bed-side of somebody else.

THE BABY'S CRADLE.

WHEN the Indian is a little baby, and can neither talk nor walk, his mother carries him about in a cradle like what you see in the picture.

What a funny kind of cradle! How different from what we have in England!

This cradle is not slung round the mother's neck, but it is kept in its place by a broad band, that passes round her head.

Do not you see this in the picture? The cradle itself is merely a piece of board, with a slip of wood at the bottom, for the baby's feet to rest on. The baby looks as if it were standing, but it is held up by those straps which pass from one side to the other of the cradle, and lace it in. One strap—or hoop, for it is made of wood—goes round its head to keep it steady.

THE BABY'S CRADLE.

THE BABY'S CRADLE.

The baby cannot move either hand or foot.

When it gets home, its mother will let its hands and arms loose. Then it can play with its playthings.

What are its playthings?

They are little tinkling coins and bits of tinsel, that shine and please the baby.

They hang down from the hoop, or strap, that keeps the baby's head in place. It will play with them for hours, and be as happy as possible.

Does the Indian mother love her baby?

Oh yes: very much indeed!

If it were to die, she would fret and grieve most sadly.

She would go about with the cradle on her back just the same.

What! when the child was gone?

Yes; she will fill it with black feathers, and carry it about for at least a year.

Sometimes, when she is at work in her house, she will lean the cradle against the side of the tent, and sit close by it. Then she will talk to it, as if her baby was inside, and say all manner of loving things to the empty cradle.

Poor mother! I am sure you are very sorry for her.

THE MEDICINE-BAG.

THE Indian has left his cradle a long time ago. When he was old enough, his mother took him out of the cradle, and let him roll about on the grass, and do just as he liked.

He was still a baby, and could neither walk nor talk. But he was strong and healthy; and he soon grew up to be a lad.

Where did his father and mother live? Sometimes in a tent, sometimes in a hut made of logs. The tent was used in summer. It was a very large tent, and held a great many people. It was called a wigwam.

How was it made?

Of the skins of buffaloes stretched on long poles, and coming to a point at the top, as you see in the picture.

The skins were very nicely dressed, for the Indian can do this well; or rather, his wife can. Most of the work falls to the lot of the women. You may see how busy they are!

When the skin is dressed, it is as soft and beautiful as possible. If it gets wet twenty times a-day it will dry just as soft as ever. The skins are stitched together to make them large enough. Sometimes they have pictures on them, of animals, and birds, and men.

THE MEDICINE-BAG.

WIGWAMS OF THE RED MEN.

When the tent had to come down, every one was very busy indeed. The poles were tied together, and dragged along by horses to the place where the Indians wanted to go.

The poor tired women are often glad to ride on the poles or on the backs of the horses. They have done all the work of taking down the tents.

The little Indian lad likes to move about. He has a very merry life of it. Sometimes he swims in the clear river, or gallops with his father over the prairie, or sits and listens to the tales of the old men, and hears how many battles they have fought, and how many enemies they have killed.

The fighting men are called warriors. They are very brave. If they were put to the greatest pain, they would never cry out. The little lad is not old enough yet to be a warrior. But the time comes at last. He is fifteen years of age, and he wants to leave off playing with the boys, and take his place among the men.

Will the grave old warriors allow him?

THE MEDICINE-BAG.

Not till he gets a medicine-bag. I will tell you how he gets his medicine-bag.

He goes into a cave quite away from his friends. Then he sits down on the floor. He means to be in that cave four days without anything to eat. He thinks the Great Spirit will be pleased with him, if he torments himself in this way.

Time passes on. In spite of his strength he begins to be faint and weary. The sun rises and sets, the moon and stars look peacefully down. Again it is morning. Yet he has neither had bit or drop. He has made up his mind to fast to the end, if it kills him.

He is lying now on the floor. His eyes are shut. This is the time when he thinks the Great Spirit will tell him how to make his medicine-bag.

He begins to doze; then he dreams a little. He has seen the great buffalo hunted on the plains, and perhaps he dreams of it. When he wakes up, he says the Great Spirit has told him to make his medicine-bag of the skin of a buffalo.

The Indians will think that the Great Spirit has spoken to him. But it is only a dream.

If he had dreamed of a dog, or a horse, or even a rat, he would have said that he must make his medicine-bag of its skin.

This is why the medicine-bags are made of all kinds of materials under the sun.

Then the poor, faint lad, weary and giddy with fasting, gets up. He staggers out of the cave, for he can hardly walk. When he reaches his tent he calls out for something to eat. His mother gives him plenty of food, and he makes a hearty meal. Then he thinks about hunting the buffalo.

He gets on his horse, and gallops off to the prairie. There he knows that he shall find plenty of buffaloes.

What great fierce-looking creatures they are! Their long shaggy hair hangs over their eyes. Their huge horns are very frightful. But the young Indian has seen the buffalo before to-day, and he knows what to do. His nimble little horse gallops much faster than the buffalo can run. He soon comes close up to it, and, in a moment, a sharp arrow is in the creature's side.

The arrow was shot from the bow of the young Indian. Another follows it quick as thought, and very soon the poor buffalo is stretched dead on the plain.

The Indian has plenty of material out of which to make his medicine-bag.

What good will his medicine-bag do him?

He thinks it will prevent the Evil Spirit from hurting him. He would not lose his medicine-bag for the world. You could not buy it of him for money. Unless, indeed, he meets with one of the good missionaries and learns to be a Christian.

Then he knows that God is Almighty, and can keep him from Evil Spirits, and guard him by night and by day.

And when he is sure of this, he will cast his medicine-bag to the winds.

THE FEAST OF GREEN CORN.

SHOULD you like to hear a little more about the red men?

There are many tribes or nations, each of which has a chief over it. The tribes have funny names: one is called "Blackfeet," another "Flathead," another "Crow," and so on.

Do they grow corn?

Yes; they grow Indian corn, or maize, as it is called.

They gather the corn and dry it to use in the winter. That is, as much of the corn as is left.

They are very fond of green corn, and boil it in kettles and eat it.

People in England would never think of being so wasteful as to eat the corn before it was ripe.

But the red man is not so careful and thrifty as his brother the white man.

As soon as the ear of corn has swelled enough, and is soft and tender,

THE FEAST OF GREEN CORN.

THE RED MAN'S CORN.

the Indian women go and feel it. If it is ready to get, they bring back word to the tents.

And then comes the feast of green corn.

Nothing is to be done for the next few days, not even fighting; and the Indian will go without food, and make himself as hungry as he can, that he may eat the more of the green corn.

When all is ready, and the corn gathered, the whole village comes to the place where the feast is to be held.

Where is the feast held?

In an open space in the middle of the village. An Indian village is nothing but a number of tents, or huts, put very near each other. A space is always left—a kind of play-ground I might call it—where the Indians have their games and dances.

Here the feast of green corn is going to be held.

A fire is made, and a kettle full of corn hung over it. This first kettleful is to be offered to the Great Spirit.

While it is boiling, a great deal of singing and dancing is going on. Four of the medicine-men, with their rattles, and with ears of corn in their hands, dance nearest to the kettle.

Then the chiefs and warriors form a larger circle, all with ears of corn in their hands, and dance, while a song of thanksgiving is sung to the Great Spirit.

It is like a harvest feast.

A number of bowls are laid on the ground, each with a spoon in it. The spoon is made of buffalo horn. The Indians are going to eat out of the bowls.

When the first kettleful of corn has been boiled enough, it is offered to the Great Spirit, and the ears of corn burned.

Then another fire is made, and the feast begins in earnest.

The chiefs eat their corn first, and then the whole tribe fall upon the young tender ears, boiled just to a turn, and devour as much as they can; and they sing and dance, and give themselves up to pleasure.

The feast lasts till all the green corn is gone, and the corn that is left in the fields has grown too ripe and too hard to be eaten with any comfort. Then, the half-stripped fields are left till the harvest.

THE BUFFALO.

GOD has taken care to provide food for all His children. Though they are of different colours and nations, they are under His protection. And it is He who opens His hand and supplies their wants.

It is He who gave the reindeer to the Laplander, and the camel to the Arab, and has filled the great sea with living creatures which serve as food for man.

There is the whale, the walrus, and the seal, all of which afford an abundant supply to the poor half-starved people who live in the Frozen Zone. And as we go on further, we shall find large juicy fruits growing in profusion, and cocoa-nuts, and dates, for those who have their home under the burning sun of the Torrid Zone.

In the vast plains or prairies of America, there are thousands and thousands of wild cattle roaming about, and yielding food to the tribes of Indians, and also to the white men.

The Indian could not live without the buffalo.

The buffalo meat is his chief food. He dries it for the winter, and feasts upon it in the summer. The buffalo skin makes his fine dresses and robes, and also his tents.

As I told you before, he can dress these skins and make them look very nice indeed. And he has plenty of practice. Everything in an Indian village is made out of "buffalo."

The Indian hunts the buffalo with his nimble little horse.

His horse came from the prairie, and once scampered about wild and free. But one day, when the Indian wanted a horse, he came to look at the wild herd in the prairie. He galloped up, and threw his lasso round the neck of the first he could reach. All the quickest of the horses were out of his sight in a moment.

The horse, that was caught, could not get away, because the more it pulled, the tighter the noose was round its throat. Then the Indian got off his own horse, and tied the two fore-legs of the one he had caught together. It soon left off struggling, and was led away by its new master and made to work.

So you see the prairie gives the Indian horses to ride upon, as well as buffaloes to hunt.

The great heavy buffalo cannot run so fast as the nimble little horse. The Indian shoots his arrow while the horse is going at full speed. But he does not often miss his aim. He has his quiver slung over his back, and arrow after arrow flies as quick as lightning.

The red man knows how to hunt the buffalo.

Sometimes a grand hunt takes place.

All the Indians of the village go out on horseback.

The great herd of buffaloes is feeding in the prairie. The Indians make a circle all round them, and then gallop furiously upon them, shooting arrows in every direction. There is a dreadful noise and dust; horses, buffaloes, and men, are all mingled in confusion. The men are so quick and clever, that if thrown off their horses, they will scramble out of the way of danger. They will even climb along the backs of the buffaloes till they have reached a place of safety.

The hunt lasts a long time, and does not end until nearly all the buffaloes have been killed. Then the hunters go away, leaving the field strewed all over with dead buffaloes.

The next day the women come to finish the work. The men think

BUFFALOES HAVING A GALLOP.

they have done enough; and they sit and smoke their pipes at home. The women go out and skin the buffaloes, and cut them up into meat. It is hard work, and they come back so loaded they can hardly crawl.

There are great rejoicings at the plenty of food that is being brought in. Sometimes the Indians dance the buffalo dance. They are very fond of dancing, as you perceive.

Each man has the great head and horns of a buffalo on his shoulders, and dances about as if he were mad. And another man will hunt him about as if he were a buffalo. When the man is tired of being hunted about, he stoops down, and then the other man shoots a blunt arrow at him. Then the man who is shot, drops down and pretends to be killed. He is dragged away, and the women brandish their knives over him, and pretend to think he is a buffalo.

The dance is danced when the buffaloes have roamed a good way off and not one of them is to be seen.

The medicine-man tells the people that they must begin to dance, and then the buffaloes will come.

So on they dance, day after day, shooting and shouting, until at last news is brought that the buffaloes are in sight.

Then the dance stops, and all the men seize their horses and set off for the hunt.

The medicine-man has a shout of thanks—cheers, we should call them. Because the poor ignorant Indian believes that the buffaloes have been danced back again.

THE INDIAN WHEN HE IS OLD.

WHEN the Indian gets an old man, he cannot go out hunting as he used to do. And he cannot fight, or dance, or go about from place to place.

He is very feeble and infirm, and wants some one to take care of him. Then what becomes of him?

The tribe to which he belongs do not very well know what to do with an old man. They are obliged to move about, and hunt, and go through a great many hardships.

Perhaps they cannot stay any longer in the place where they are. Then I will tell you what they do.

They make a little shed or hut for the poor old man, so that he may have a shelter. And they give him a little meat and a vessel of water.

And then they bid him good-bye.

Are they going to leave him?

Yes. All alone in the wilderness, with no one to speak to or to be kind to him. And with howling wolves on every side.

How very dreadful!

It is dreadful. People in Christian countries are shocked to think of it. But the Indians are used to forsake their parents if they live to be old. The poor old man had very likely left his father in the same way.

He does not make any trouble of being left. He tells his children to go and take care of themselves. He knows he is a burden to them, and will be better out of the way.

A traveller will sometimes come upon a little hut of skins, standing quite by itself.

What will he see inside?

Nothing but a few bones.

He feels very sad. He knows that he has come to a place where some poor old man has been left.

THE PRAIRIE ON FIRE.

Do you see those red streaks in the sky? I wonder where they come from! Volumes of smoke keep rolling on, and there is a queer, crackling noise. The noise seems to get nearer and nearer; and now it rolls along with a mighty sound like thunder. On come, the red leaping flames. It is easy to see what is the matter—

The prairie is on fire!

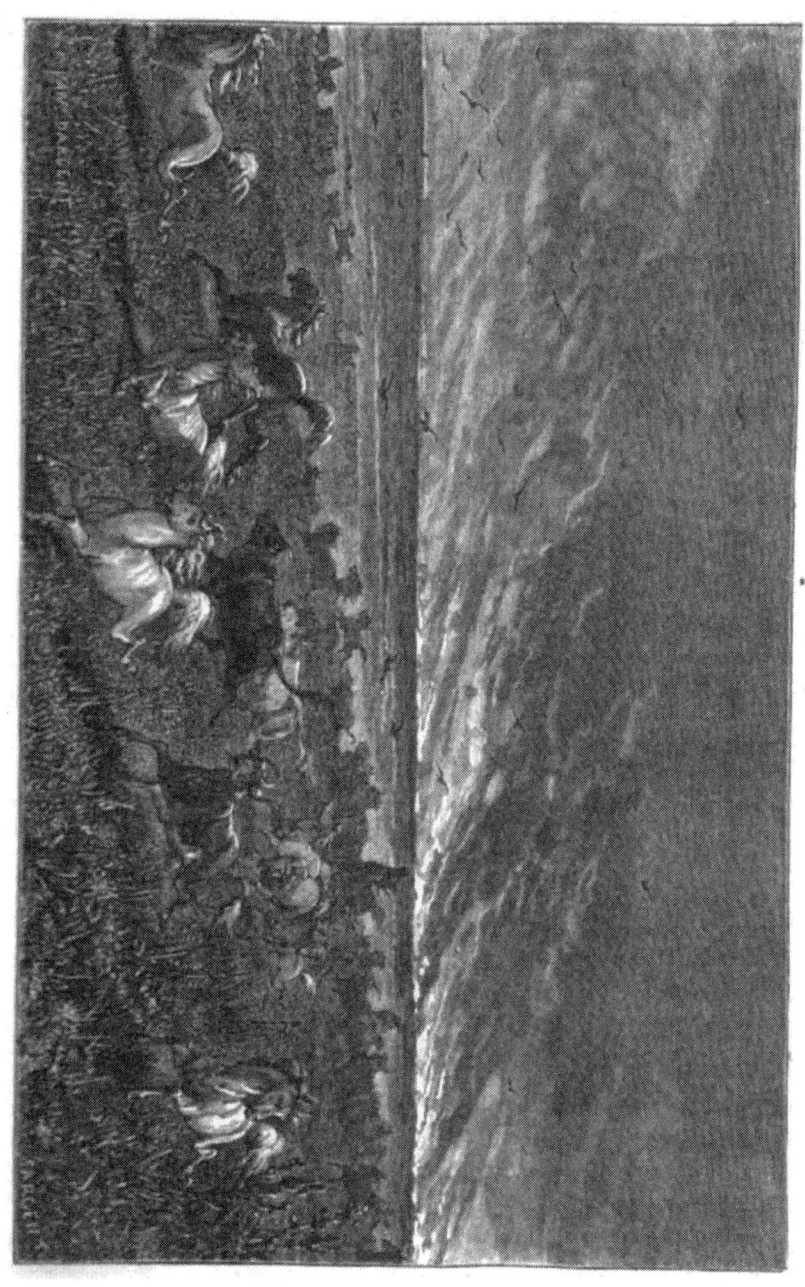

THE PRAIRIE ON FIRE.

What is the prairie?

It is an immense plain or common that reaches for miles and miles. Long waving grass grows in it. It is like a waving sea of grass.

Where is the prairie?

The prairie in the picture is in North America. It is the place where the Indian fetches his horses from, and where he hunts his buffaloes.

How many things there are in this vast country!

Mighty rivers; deep forests; and now the rolling, far-spreading prairie.

Birds and animals make their home in the prairie. The wild horse gallops about with its mane flowing in the wind. The fierce buffalo is there. The wolves roam about in packs. There is plenty of food for them all.

The wolf does not eat grass. He preys on the smaller animals; and seizes and tears to pieces whatever falls in his way. He even attacks a wild horse, or a buffalo, if it is weak or old, and cannot keep up with the rest. The eagle and the vulture hover in the air, and find something to pounce down upon and devour.

But now a terrible fright has seized the wild beasts of the prairie.

The long waving grass is on fire!

I cannot tell who has done the mischief. Perhaps an Indian left his fire burning, or dropped a spark from his pipe; or the dry weather has lasted a long time, and the grass takes fire of its own accord. At any rate, the mischief is done. If men are at hand, they try to stop the fire by burning a large space all round where they stand. When the fire gets to the bare place it stops. There is nothing more for it to burn. But such a fire as this, has got beyond the power of any one to stop.

What becomes of the poor animals?

They have but one way of escape, and that is by flight.

The horses gallop madly along—their eyes starting, their manes flowing. The buffaloes are not so swift, but they make all the haste they can. Each tries to shift for himself. Each knows, by instinct, that the red scorching flames are coming to devour him.

There is scarcely anything in this part of the world so terrible, and so out of the power of man to control, as the prairie on fire!

THE HERONS IN THE CEDAR SWAMP.

HERONS ON THE TREE TOPS.

In the sad old days, the white men in America used to buy the black man for money, and make him a slave. Then the black man used often to run away from his master, and hide himself in the cedar swamp.

What is the cedar swamp?

It is a very dreary place. You can call it a forest, if you like.

It is full of tall trees, that stand so close together you could hardly get between them. The trunks of the trees are quite bare, for all the branches grow at the top.

The branches are so matted together, that you cannot see the sky. And when the wind blows, the tall stems sway about, and rattle one against the other, and make the most dismal noise you can imagine.

THE HERONS IN THE CEDAR SWAMP.

It is scarcely possible for a man to make his way through the cedar swamp.

It is called swamp, because the ground under foot is soft like a bog, and if any one tries to walk there, he sinks up to his knees at every step.

Great logs of fallen trees block up the way, and thick bushes of laurel fill up every bit of room. He has to squeeze through the bushes, and clamber over the logs, and wade through the bog.

Besides this, he has to swim over pools of water, where the alligator is lurking in the mud. For the alligator loves the gloom and darkness of the cedar swamp.

There is a long-legged bird, called a heron, which loves the swamp as well as the alligator.

There are many kinds of herons, but this is the night-heron. Like the owl, he flies about in the night.

Every spring, a great flock of herons come to the swamp. They fly to their old nests, on the top of the tallest trees. The young birds who have no nests set to work to make them.

The nests are made of sticks, and lined with twigs and wool. They are so large that only one nest can be built on a single tree.

The mother heron lays four eggs, a little bigger than hen's eggs.

When the young herons are a few weeks old, they begin to climb about the branches. But they do not fly till they are nearly grown up.

When night comes, the herons sally out to find something to eat.

There is plenty of food for them in the ponds and creeks of water.

They catch fish, and frogs, and insects, and anything that comes in their way.

The heron wades into the water, and stands there, looking for a fish to come swimming by.

The moment the fish comes near enough, the heron pounces upon it with his long bill, and devours it.

The frogs are sharper than the fishes. They dive into the mud, and lie there quite still, until they think the heron is gone.

But the heron is as cunning as they are. He does not mean to go.

THE HERONS IN THE CEDAR SWAMP.

He sees the spot where the frog has gone down into the mud, and he comes close to it. He does not make the slightest noise with his feet, lest the frog should hear him.

But there he stands watching.

He is very patient when he is watching for his food.

He stands so long, that the frog thinks he must be gone. And it puts out its silly little head to look.

Then down comes the great strong bill of the heron, and there is an end of the poor frog.

The heron has an excellent appetite, and can eat a great many fishes and frogs. When he has had enough, he goes

HERONS FISHING IN A SWAMP.

SIR WALTER RALEIGH AND HIS TWO PLANTS.

back to his swamp, and stands on one leg till he has digested his supper.

The Indians admire the long flowing feathers of the heron, and wear them on their heads for an ornament.

SIR WALTER RALEIGH AND HIS TWO PLANTS.

PEOPLE in England did without tea for a very long time. And for a long time, they did without potatoes.

Where did the potato come from?

From North America. Sir Walter Raleigh first brought it to England in the reign of Queen Elizabeth.

He brought another plant as well, which is not half so useful. I mean the tobacco-plant.

THE TOBACCO PLANT.

He had seen the Indians smoke, and he thought he should like to try. So he found out all about tobacco, and learned to smoke it.

A funny story is told about Sir Walter Raleigh and his cigar.

When he got back to his own house in England, and was sitting over the fire, he began to smoke. In the middle of his smoking the door opened and in came his servant-man.

Now, this man had never seen any one smoke in his life, and did not know there was such a plant as tobacco.

When he saw the smoke coming from his master's mouth, he thought he was on fire.

He cried out in a fright, and ran to fetch a bucket of water to put out the fire. Before Sir Walter had time to explain, he was deluged with water, and his clothes were wet through.

But very soon the old servant got used to seeing people with smoke coming out of their mouths, and all the young nobles of the court began to smoke because Sir Walter did. And from the very first, the tobacco was made a great fuss with.

How did people like the potato?

Not at all. Nobody would eat it. Yet Sir Walter told them how useful it would be. The potato, he said, could be made to grow in England. The tobacco will not grow anywhere but in a hot country. And when the corn-harvest failed, which it often used to do, people need not starve if they had plenty of potatoes. Queen Elizabeth, who was a very clever woman, listened to what Sir Walter said. And she had potatoes served up at her own table. The grand people, who dined with her majesty, were obliged to eat them. But they went away and spread a report that the potato was poisonous.

THE POTATO PLANT.

They said so, because the potato belongs to the same order as the deadly nightshade and many other poisonous plants. And they could not believe it was wholesome. So, in spite of all that Queen Elizabeth could do, no one would eat potatoes, and they were left for the pigs.

When did people find out their mistake?

Not till many years after. The poor potato was despised and forgotten till the reign of the French king, Louis XVI.

A man lived in this reign, who was very clever in growing plants for food. He felt sure he could make the potato a great blessing to the country. And he set about to try.

Did he succeed?

After a great deal of trouble he did. People laughed at him, and would not take any notice of what he said. But he went on growing the potato till he had brought it to perfection. Even then, no one would have eaten it, if the king had not taken its part. The king had large pieces of ground planted with potatoes. And he went about with the flower of the potato in his button-hole.

No one dare laugh at the king; and when he said potatoes were to be eaten, people began to find out how good and wholesome they were.

By degrees the potato was more and more liked. In these days there is no vegetable that is so highly thought of. We could never do without the potato.

What was the name of the wise Frenchman who would grow the potato?

We ought never to forget it.

His name was Parmentier.

THE WILD PIGEONS OF AMERICA.

A vast army of pigeons makes its home in the forests of America.

If you went into the forest where they live, you would find the trees beaten down and broken. Great branches lie strewed on the ground. And the ground is as much trampled down, as if an army of soldiers had been there.

The pigeons have done all the mischief.

When they have eaten up all the nuts and acorns, and every bit of

THE WILD PIGEONS OF AMERICA.

WILD PIGEONS.

fruit they can find, and have destroyed as much as they have eaten, they go to another place.

The whole army of pigeons rises into the air with a rushing noise like thunder.

They fly so high that nobody can shoot them.

Once, a man was sailing down the river, and he went on shore to get something to eat. While he was in the shop, there came a rushing noise that was just like a hurricane. He thought it was a hurricane, and that the house was going to be blown down.

But the man he was talking to merely said, "Ah! there are the pigeons."

It was a very wonderful sight. The air was full of pigeons. On they swept by—and on—and on. There seemed no end to them. Their wings shone and glistened in the sun; and looked now green, and now purple, and kept changing colour every minute.

For three days this army of pigeons kept flying past.

It was a mile in breadth; and it was two hundred and forty miles long!

The rushing noise made by the wings of the pigeons was so great, that horses on the road took fright, and people could hardly hear themselves speak.

When the pigeons reach the part of the forest to which they are going, they rush in with a tremendous noise. They soon batter down the branches with their wings, and make a scene of ruin like what they have left.

Do people try to catch the pigeons?

Yes. When they know the pigeons are on the wing, they turn out with their guns and try to shoot them.

They can only shoot the pigeons when they come to the ground to pick up nuts and acorns.

Then they shoot so many that they get quite tired of eating them for dinner.

Indeed, the very name of the pigeon is disliked.

THE BEAVER.

THE beaver would have been left to build his house in peace if it were not for his fur coat.

The Indian thinks his flesh very nice to eat, and every now and then has a feast of it. But the Indian would never have cared to kill more beavers than he wanted for his own use.

But the white man found out that the skin of the beaver was a famous thing to make hats of—yes, and bonnets too—for those who liked them very warm.

When beaver hats began to be worn, the Indians were paid money to bring as many beaver skins as they could.

For a long time the poor beaver had very little rest for his enemies.

It was in vain he made his house as strong as he could. The Indian was always on the watch to break in upon him; and if he tried to swim away, the spear of the Indian would be sure to wound him. In fact, thousands of beavers fell victims to the hat-makers every year.

In these days silk hats are worn a great deal, and the beaver trade is not so brisk as it used to be.

THE BEAVER.

BEAVERS.

What kind of a house does the beaver make?

It is a house by the water; and is built of mud and stones, and branches of trees.

A great many beavers live together, and build their houses all at once. The beaver is very fond of company.

But he does not like the water to get into his house. He seems to know that if a great deal of rain came, the water would rise and swim him and his friends away. So he sets to work to prevent such a misfortune.

You cannot think how clever he is. He makes a fence across the stream just as a man might do. The fence is made of thick stakes of wood driven into the bed of the river. This stops the water when it gets high, and will not let it rush on to the house of the beaver.

All the beavers work at the fence, and do not rest until it is done. They use their sharp teeth instead of a saw, and get on so fast that the fence is soon finished. When all is safe, they begin to make their houses.

What do the beavers live upon?

They eat the roots of a kind of water-lily, that grows at the bottom of the water; and they gnaw the bark of trees, and devour berries, and herbs, and what else they can find. In the summer they cut sticks and pieces of wood with their sharp teeth, and lay them before their houses.

This is done that they may have something to eat in the winter.

The little beavers are very fond of play. They make a cry something like that of a child. A gentleman once saw a number of little beavers at play. He crept towards them with his gun in his hand, ready to shoot. But their pretty gambols, and the cry they made, reminded him of his children at home. He could not find it in his heart to shoot; and, I am happy to say, he left the little beavers to have their gambols in peace.

THE MAHOGANY TREE.

A VERY great tree grows in America. It grows near the Bay of Honduras. It has a thick solid trunk, and wide-spreading arms. Its leaves are a shining green, and it bears little white flowers.

This tree takes a long time to grow. It does not come to its full size in the lifetime of a man. It is called the mahogany tree.

Do you mean the mahogany like our chairs and tables?

Yes. Once, people did not know anything about mahogany.

Sir Walter Raleigh went a great many voyages in the days of Queen Elizabeth. He brought part of a mahogany tree from America, and had his ships mended with it.

He thought it a very fine wood. But there were so many fine things in the New World, that the mahogany was passed over.

A long time after this, it chanced that a few boards came to England in a ship. The captain of the ship had a brother who was a doctor.

The doctor was building a house, and he thought he would use the boards to make his doors of.

He tried to use it, but the workmen said the wood was so hard it spoiled their tools.

So, after all, only a piece of the mahogany was used, and that was made into a candle-box.

But the candle-box looked so handsome when it was done, that every one who saw it admired it.

And people began to think what a fine wood this mahogany was.

Very soon the maker of the candle-box had enough to do.

All his customers wanted furniture made of the new wood. And you will not wonder that he made his fortune as well.

How do people get the mahogany?

It grows in the forests, and the black men are sent to cut it down. A black man climbs up the tallest tree he can find. Then he looks round to see how many mahogany trees are growing there. He knows them by their reddish colour. Then he points them out to the other negroes, and they set to work to cut them down. When the trees are felled and cut into logs, the negroes make a raft of them, and float them all down the river. When they get to the sea, ships are ready to take them to Europe.

WHERE DOES THE COTTON COME FROM?

THE COTTON PLANT.

THERE is scarcely anything we see about us so common as cotton. We meet with it everywhere.

In the great town of Manchester there are warehouses and factories full of cotton. In the shop windows you can see cotton gowns by hundreds. People use cotton, and wear cotton, every day of their lives.

I wonder where all the cotton comes from.

Not from England; though a very clever man once said that it would grow anywhere.

Grow? What! is it a plant?

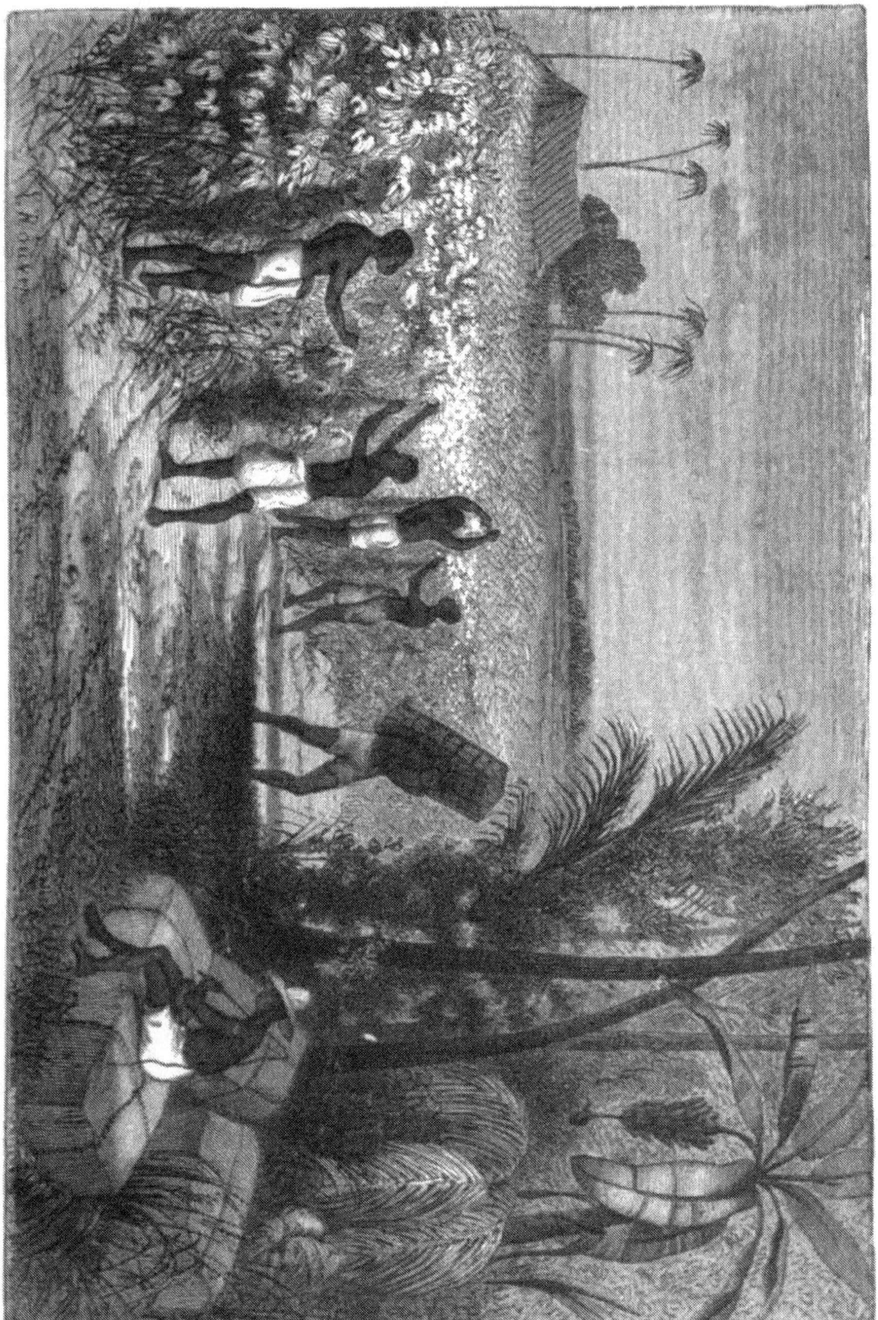

6

Yes, it is a plant. All the cotton in the warehouses and in the shops, once grew on a shrub.

The shrub grows in many countries. It grows in America, and in India, and in China, and in Persia, and in Sicily.

A writer who lived in very old times, when Great Britain was overgrown with forests, speaks of the cotton tree. He says:

"There is a plant which does not bear fruit, but cotton; and the people make their clothes of it."

Do you see the flower of the cotton tree? It is white, and the leaves are a dark glossy green. The seed or pod bursts when it is ripe, and then the owner of the cotton plantation knows that it is time to bestir himself.

Then, women and children come into the plantation before the sun rises. If the sun shines on the cotton it will turn yellow. Sometimes they take off the whole of the pod just as it is. In other places, they take out the cotton and leave the pod behind.

Look at the pod in the picture. It has burst, and that is the cotton ready to be gathered.

How does the cotton look when it is in the pod?

Not as it does in the shop windows, of course. It is merely the rough material which Nature gives us.

The cotton now looks like a white pulp, and is mixed with the seeds that have come with it out of the pod.

The first thing to be done is to get the cotton away from the seeds. This is very tiresome to do, and takes a long time, if the men do it by hand. That is, without the help of a machine.

In India, all the cotton is picked by hand. A man can only do about a pound of cotton in a day. This is very slow work indeed.

In other places people use machines. In America, the cotton-planters have a very large machine. It can cleanse, or separate from the seeds, eight or nine hundred pounds of cotton a-day.

What a difference between the two ways!

In England we have machines of all kinds. When the cotton comes to us, we can have it made into cloth very quickly indeed.

Manchester is a famous place for cotton. Some years ago it was quite a village. Cotton did not come to England in such quantities then; for it had to be spun by hand, and we did not use so much.

But a clever man invented a machine to spin it, and then people could get it for less money.

Cotton comes to us now from all parts of the world. And as our steam-ships fly across the waves, they bring it very quickly. I will give you some idea of how fast the machines do their work. A man had ten large bales or bundles of raw cotton come to him. The bales were taken into the top-rooms of his factory. They were moved down by degrees from one story to another. In one story they were carded, then spun, then woven. By the end of ten days the cotton had travelled down to the lowest story of all.

Not in bales! Oh no!

It was now a white strong cloth, ready to be made up.

THE SUGAR-CANE.

THE sugar that tastes so nice in your tea comes a long way off.

It comes from a plant called a sugar-cane. You see in the picture what kind of a plant it is. It grows like a cane, and has a bunch of leaves at the top. It is really a grass, though it does not look much like one.

Where does the sugar-cane grow? In countries where it is very hot. The monkeys and the humming-birds live in that country. The sun pours down his rays so fiercely that you could not bear it a moment.

But the black people do not mind the heat so much as we do. See how busy they are!

They are cutting down the canes, and tying them in bundles. The canes are quite ripe, and are full of a sweet juice, which is going to be made into sugar. To squeeze this juice out, the canes are put into a mill.

GATHERING THE SUGAR-CANES.

THE SUGAR-CANE.   87

The mill is nothing more than two great rollers, and as the juice is squeezed out, it runs into a kind of cistern beneath.

Then, it has to be boiled directly, or else it goes sour.

The juice becomes a thick syrup with being boiled. It is put into

THE SUGAR-CANE.

shallow basins to get cool. As it cools, it becomes sugar. When the sugar is made it is packed into great tubs called hogsheads. But it is not yet quite clear. Holes are pierced in the bottom of the tubs, and a thick substance like treacle drains away. The thick substance is called molasses.

When this is done, the sugar is ready to be shipped off to other countries. The black people who made the sugar used to be slaves. A cruel man drove them to work with a whip. But now they are all free men.

If you look on the map, you will find a group of islands called the

West Indies. One of these islands belongs to England. It is called Jamaica. It is a very lovely island indeed. The air is sweet with spices. Birds of the brightest colours flit among the trees. But it was not a happy island while it was full of slaves. The slaves were made to work hard among the sugar-canes, and were bought and sold like cattle. But, thank God! there are no slaves now. The sugar-cane grows in America. And here were slaves to dig, and hoe, and cut the bundles of canes, and get out the sugar.

But in America there are no slaves now. All have been set free. Where do the slaves come from?

From Africa. I am sorry to tell you, that men went in ships on purpose to steal them.

WHERE DOES COCOA COME FROM?

Do you ever drink cocoa?

People who think that tea does them harm, and keeps them awake at night, are glad to take cocoa.

Cocoa is thicker than coffee, and has a great deal of support in it.

COCOA SEED

Travellers often take little cakes of cocoa with them on their journeys. When they are hungry, and cannot get anything to eat, they are in no danger of starving, if they have plenty of cocoa.

Cocoa is often called chocolate.

Where does cocoa come from?

It comes from Mexico.

It is made from the seeds of a tree called the Cacao, or the Chocolate Tree.

The Chocolate Tree is very easy to make grow. It has a smooth gray bark, and large oval leaves, and clusters of pale pink flowers.

HARVEST OF THE COCOA IN MEXICO.

WHERE DOES COCOA COME FROM?

When the fruit is fully grown, it becomes of a red-brown colour. It is full of seeds placed in rows. These seeds are what the cocoa is made of.

All round the seeds is a soft pulpy substance that has a pleasant acid taste. The people of Mexico eat it with sugar, as we should an orange.

Those Indians who are too lazy to take any trouble, eat the pulp, and throw the seeds away.

In places where these lazy Indians set up a camp, heaps of seeds are found lying about and wasted.

But the man who wishes to make himself and his family well off, will not throw away seeds that are precious almost as gold.

He will plant chocolate trees round his house. They will have to be shaded from the sun; and to do this he will set banana trees close by them. The banana will throw a cool and pleasant shadow, and also give him plenty of food. He can live on his bananas while the chocolate plants are growing.

His chocolate plants do not flower for some years, and this is the worst part of the story. But he must have patience, and take care that the caterpillars do not eat them. When the fruit does come, flocks of parrots will settle on the trees, to feast on the nice soft pulp.

If he does not mind, they will run away with all his fruit.

But if he has been careful, and picked off the caterpillars, and driven away the parrots, he will have a famous crop.

His trees will have had all the lower branches taken off, and they will form the most delightful walks; and the long rows of trees, all loaded with fruit, will rejoice his heart.

He will begin to think that it is time to have his fruit gathered.

Then will come a negro, with a forked wooden stick. He will pull off the fruit with the stick, and then another negro will carry it off to a shed.

Some old negroes and some women, who cannot do very hard work, are in the shed. They are going to take out the seeds.

They cut the fruit open, and then take out the seeds with a wooden spoon.

The seeds are not quite clear from the pulp. They are put into a hole, and covered with fine sand. This is done to get out all the moisture.

The seeds are then spread on mats in the sun to get perfectly dry.

How big are the seeds?

About an inch long. Some seeds are larger than others.

When the seeds are quite dry, they are packed in bags made of the hide of the buffalo, and sent to all parts of Europe and America.

Are they ready for use?

No. They have to be roasted like coffee-berries, and then they are crushed under a roller till they become a fine powder. A little sugar and spice are added, and a little water.

Then the cocoa is pressed into packets, such as you see in the shops.

THE FOREST IN BRAZIL.

You cannot fancy anything half so wonderful as the forest in the picture. There is nothing like it in England; no, nor in all Europe.

There are trees in this forest which are taller than the tallest church steeple. Quite deep in the forest, they grow so thick together, and there are so many shrubs, that no one can get through, except it is the Indian, for he can make his way where a white man cannot.

Do you see those curious plants that hang down from the branches of the trees like cords or streamers? They are called vegetable cables, because they are so much like ropes. They wind round and round the trees for miles and miles. The monkeys run along them merrily. Great rivers run through the forest. In America everything is great. Great mountains, great rivers, and great forests.

There is a little stream or creek almost hidden by the gigantic ferns and shrubs. Some of the Indians are swimming or wading along. It is easier to find a path along the water, when the forest is so thick, than on the land.

What Indians are they?

THE FOREST IN BRAZIL.

FOREST IN BRAZIL.

They belong to the great family of Indians who lived in America when the white man came.

They live scattered about, some in villages, some in solitary huts, some in the forest. They have not the same habits as the red men of the north. They do not depend so much on hunting. In this hot climate, there are plenty of fruits. The plantain and the banana both supply the Indian with food. One cluster of bananas will yield as many as a hundred and sixty fruits. The fruit is very sweet and nice, and stands in the place of bread. If the Indian has a little plot of bananas round his hut, he will not trouble himself to grow anything else. Like his brother in the north, he would do anything rather than work.

When he wants to hunt the wild beasts, or to fight, he takes his bow and arrow.

His arrows are often deadly, because they are tipped with poison. Where does he get the poison from? From one of the plants that grows in the forest. It is called mandioc, and serves him for food as well as for poison.

The plant grows about as high as a man, and has a twisted stem, covered with knots or bumps. The wife of the Indian digs up the roots while her husband lies down at his ease, and smokes his pipe.

He wears very little clothing in this hot country. But he will have a plume of feathers on his head, and his knife in his girdle.

He is quite content to be idle, and to let his wife work for him.

She is as busy as can be. When she has dug, or rather drawn, the roots of mandioc out of the ground, she washes them, and then pounds them with a wooden club till they are a thick pulp.

She will put the pulp into a bag made of a great leaf, and hang it on a stick over the fire. A heavy stone is hung to the bottom of the bag, and very soon the juice begins to run out. It runs into a gourd that is set to catch it.

This juice is the deadly poison, and as it drops, the wife keeps dipping her husband's arrows into it.

When the juice has stood a long time it is quite clear, and a white powder, like starch, is at the bottom of the gourd. The wife pours off the poison, and washes the fine powder in water.

It is ready then, to be made into a cake, and used for food.

The white people in Brazil use this white powder as we do flour. They have mills to grind it, instead of preparing it in the rude way the Indian does.

The flour is called farinha. Almost every dish on the table is partly made of farinha.

It is the staple food of Brazil.

THE INDIAN'S DRINKING FEAST.

The Indian likes, now and then, to have a drinking feast.

He does not eat anything at the feast, but he will sit and drink for two or three days together.

What does he drink?

A strong liquor made from the root of the mandioc.

He does not make it himself. There is a saying among the Indians, that the banqueting drink, as it is called, must be made by the hands of women.

How do the women make it?

In a way that we should not think very nice. Indeed, we should not like to touch it.

The women slice the roots of the mandioc, and boil them till they are quite soft.

When the roots are cool, the women set to work to chew them. Then they put out the chewed roots into a vessel of water, that stands close by. When they have chewed all the roots, the whole contents of the vessel are boiled up, and stirred while boiling.

When the liquor has been boiled long enough, it is poured into a number of jars, and buried in the floor of the house.

The mouths of the jars have been tightly stopped, and in a few days the liquor begins to ferment.

Soon after, it is thought ready to be used, and then the drinking feast begins.

The women make a fire close by the jars to warm up the liquor. Then the men come, dancing and singing, to the house, and the women serve out the drink in cups made of a gourd.

When the jars are all emptied in one house the Indians go to another. And so they go on drinking, till every drop of the liquor is gone.

What a bad use to make of the mandioc root! It is as if the Indian were trying to poison himself, as well as his arrows!

THE TAPIR.

THOUGH the Indian does not like trouble, he will take a great deal sometimes. He will have a field of mandioc near his hut.

But the wild beasts of the forest like mandioc as well as the Indian. They will come trampling into his field in the night, and eat as many plants as they can.

So the Indian has to keep watch, or his harvest will be a very poor one.

Do you see the animal in the picture? He has a great snout like a pig, and is fond of eating leaves and fruit, and rooting about in the forest. If he kept in the forest, it would be all very well. But he will come stealing into the mandioc fields of the Indian.

The tapir, for this is the name of the creature, does not come out except at night. The Indian knows this, and it is at night he goes to look for him.

He can guess which way the tapir will come, for he is very clever at finding out the track of animals.

Then, he makes a little shelf to stand on, between two trees, and gets upon it.

He has his gun in his hand, or else his bow and arrow. And he stands there, hour after hour, waiting.

Nothing can tire out the patience of an Indian!

THE JAGUAR AND THE TAPIR.

THE TAPIR.

He dare not stir; for the tapir has ears as quick as a cat's ears. And treads softly, as the cat does, and can only be heard by the faint rustle of the leaves as he pushes his way through.

At length, the Indian hears the rustle, and he knows the tapir is coming.

THE TAPIR.

But the creature must come near enough to be shot at.

If he is shot but not killed, he will defend himself with great bravery, and there will be quite a battle.

But the Indian gets the best of it. He either kills the tapir or drives him away.

The flesh of the tapir is very good to eat, for animals as well as for men.

The fierce jaguar likes to fling himself on the tapir and devour him.

But the tapir has no notion of being eaten. He will set off at full speed, and drag the jaguar with him. And he will push through such rough thorny places, and thick bushes, that the jaguar is scratched almost to death. And at last, he is obliged to leave go, and let the tapir get away.

A LITTLE ABOUT BRAZIL.

You will see what a great country Brazil is, by looking at it on the map.

Thirty-five Great Britains joined together would only make one Brazil.

It is a very glorious country. Plenty of rain falls there, to make the grass and herbs grow. There are mighty rivers, and high mountains, and mines of gold and silver.

There are no deserts in Brazil. No cutting winds sweep over it. The climate is pleasant. There are no earthquakes to shake down the towns and cities.

It is a favoured land, well watered, and rich, and fertile.

What people live in Brazil?

White men, black men, and Indians. The white men are descended from the Spaniards and the Portuguese. The black men are negroes.

Many of the negroes used to be slaves. But a slave can now buy his own freedom if he likes to work for it. Very soon, there will be no slaves at all in Brazil.

The Indians are said to be civilized—that is, they live in houses, and mix with the white people, which the red man of the north never will.

But the Indian's nature is the same. He still loves to get away and live in the forest, where he need not be troubled to learn anything. So there are quite as many wild Indians as civilized ones.

Some descendants of the old Spanish grandees have come to poverty and live in the forest as well.

Humboldt, the great traveller, met with a family who had long-sounding names, and thought a great deal of themselves. They were far too proud to work; and how do you think they lived?

They had no house at all. They hung their hammocks in the trees, and when night came, got into them to sleep.

TREES IN BRAZIL.

It was not a very safe bed. In the middle of the night, the traveller heard a jaguar sharpening its claws against a tree; and a poor little dog, that lay on the ground, was carried off.

Is Brazil a free country?

Yes. Once it belonged to Portugal. Now it has an emperor of its own. His name is Don Pedro the Second.

You will be glad to hear that the emperor is very wise and learned, and is trying to do a great deal of good.

What is the religion of Brazil?

Roman Catholic.

THE INDIAN'S BOW AND ARROW.

WHAT a very great bow the Indian shoots with!

He lies down on the ground, and bends the bow with his feet. His quiver, full of arrows, lies beside him. He is shooting at the birds you see flying in the air. I do not think he will miss his aim. The Indian seldom does.

Shooting is one of the things he is very expert in.

Sometimes he shoots the turtle.

What! when it is in the sea?

Yes. The turtle dives and swims, and is quite below the surface of the water.

When it has to come up to breathe, it shows the tip of its nose.

It makes a ripple so slight that few people would notice it.

But the Indian's eyes are very keen. He says to himself,—

"That is the turtle, I am going to shoot!"

How does he shoot it?

He sends his arrow straight up into the air.

If he shot it sideways, it would glance off the smooth shell of the turtle, and do it no harm.

THE INDIAN'S BOW AND ARROW.

INDIAN'S WAY OF SHOOTING.

But when the arrow has gone up into the air to a great height, it turns over, and comes down again, just on the back of the turtle. It strikes the shell with a very hard blow, and makes a hole in it.

The turtle is wounded, and dives under water.

The Indian has a clever contrivance in order to make sure of the turtle.

The sharp point of the arrow is like a peg. It comes out, and is carried off by the turtle. The cord, that held the peg in its place, unwinds very quickly. It was wound round and round the arrow, to the very top. When it is all unwound, the feathery part of the arrow floats on the water.

The Indian jumps into his canoe, and rows to it. Then he pulls the cord, and draws the turtle towards him.

Of course the turtle is soon pulled into the boat, and then the Indian carries it off as a prize.

THE MONKEY BRIDGE.

THE Monkey is not very fond of coming to the ground. His long arms are given him to climb with. With his long fingers he takes hold of one bough and then another, and makes his way among the trees of the forest. He is so nimble, that we say, "as nimble as a monkey."

The trees are so matted together that he can go a great many miles without stopping. But one thing is apt to stop him. That thing is a river.

Great rivers run through the forest. The trees stand on each side of the bank, and what is the monkey to do?

He has a great many other monkeys with him, and they all come to a stand-still, as if they were consulting.

There is often a grave old monkey in the group, who acts as the leader. Perhaps he gives his advice, for there is chattering and noise enough, and they seem to be talking the matter over. At any rate, they make up their minds to cross the river.

But monkeys cannot swim. If they tried to swim, they would be drowned. But they are too cunning to do anything of the kind. You see what they are doing. There is no bridge to be had, so they make one of their own bodies.

Make a bridge of their bodies?

Yes. Watch a moment and you will see.

First one monkey takes fast hold of the tree. He holds it by his hands, and his feet, and his tail, and clutches it with all his might.

The next monkey links himself to his friend, as you may see, and holds fast by his feet and his tail. Then the next monkey does the same, and so on, till the chain is long enough to reach across the river. The last monkey in the chain, and indeed all the monkeys together swing themselves, with a great jerk, towards the tree on the opposite bank. The last monkey in the chain grasps the tree, and holds on as fast as he can.

The bridge is now made, and the rest of the monkeys, who have been looking on, begin to cross it. Of course, if it breaks down, they go into the water. And monkeys are so fond of play and mischief, that they can hardly keep quiet while their friends pass over. There is a good deal of pinching and scratching, even in this moment of danger.

At length, however, the monkeys get safely over, and the bridge swings itself after them.

THE WARRIOR ANT.

THE ants in the picture are coming home from battle.

They marched out one night in an army. They were in perfect order, like a body of soldiers.

They were going to another hillock, where some other ants were living.

The other ants saw them coming, and seemed to know what was going

THE WARRIOR ANT.

to happen. They ran to the entrance of the hillock, and tried to drive them back.

But the warrior ants knocked them over, and forced their way into the hillock.

The hillock is, as you know, full of chambers and passages. In one chamber, there lie all the eggs, and grubs or maggots, that by and by will come into ants. There is a store of food in this chamber, ready for the young ants to eat.

Some of the warrior ants snatch it up, and carry it away. But this is not all they came for. They are going to run away with the eggs, and the young grubs themselves.

They take them up without hurting them.

AFTER BATTLE.

And when they have got as many as they can, they march home again, carrying their booty with them.

You may see in the picture that one of them is pushing along a ball of white maggots. In fact, they have brought away everything they could find in the hillock, and left it a scene of desolation.

What are they going to do with the grubs?

The minute they reach home a number of ants, like so many servants, come out to meet them. These carry the grubs in-doors, and feed, and warm, and cherish them as if they were their own. In due time the grubs become ants.

What happens to them then?

They become the servants or slaves of their masters, the warrior ants. It is said, they will do everything for them, and even carry them about.

These ants live in a great many parts of the world.

They are called Amazon ants, because they are so fond of fighting.

THE ENEMY OF THE ANTS.

WHEN the ants are marching along in a body, as they do in these hot countries, they little think that an enemy is at hand.

This enemy is the great ant-eater.

He is called great, because he is so much bigger than his relations the ant-eaters who live in other parts of the world.

He is on the watch for the ants.

He has a long narrow tongue, and he lays it down on the ground just in the path of the ants.

The ants march on to it, but there they stick. The tongue is all over a sticky substance, like bird-lime, that holds them fast. Then, they are drawn into his mouth and swallowed.

Do you see the ant-eater's claws?

When he walks, the claws on his fore-feet are doubled backwards. This gives him a slow and awkward movement.

But his claws are famous weapons, and he makes good use of them.

The ants are not safe from him, even when they are snugly shut up in their ant-hill at home.

The ant-eater comes and batters and tears, with his claws, at the walls of the hillock. He soon makes a hole, and then he pushes in his long sticky tongue. The poor ants are in a sad fright. They come running out in a hurry, and of course run on the tongue of the ant-eater. He draws them into his mouth, and in this way he gets a good feast of ants.

THE GREAT ANT-EATER.

The Indians ought to thank the ant-eater for getting rid of some of the ants. But they often hunt him, because they think his flesh is good to eat.

He cannot run very fast, and if it begins to rain he will stand still, and turn his bushy tail over his head like an umbrella. The Indian is a cunning hunter. He will make a pattering noise, as if rain were falling on the leaves. The ant-eater stands still, and thinks it is raining. Then the Indian soon comes up with him, and kills him.

It is not very safe to go near the ant-eater's claws. He can fight with them, and give very hard blows.

He is sometimes a match for the jaguar. He seizes hold of him with his claws, and makes great wounds in his sides.

When the ant-eater goes to sleep, he rolls himself round like a ball, and is quite covered by his bushy tail. Rolled up in this manner, he looks very much like a bundle of hay.

LEAVES WALKING.

A TRAVELLER was one day looking about him in the forest. He saw, what seemed to him, a number of leaves walking. The leaves were cut into round pieces the size of a sixpence, and on they marched as if they had legs.

Each piece of a leaf was carried by an ant.

What were the ants going to do with the leaves?

They were carrying them off to their houses.

Their houses were hillocks something like what the mole makes, only a great deal wider round. They were full of long winding passages, and at the entrance of the passages was a little porch to keep the rain from getting in. The porch was thatched with leaves.

In that country the rain, when it does come, pours in torrents, and the ants did not want the little grubs to get wet.

Where are the houses?

In the forests. But the ant is not contented with the trees that grow wild in the forest. It will take a journey to the gardens, or to the places where coffee-plants are growing.

It will cut pieces out of the leaves, and do a great deal of mischief.

It is very curious to see the ant getting the leaves.

A great many ants climb up the tree. They are very large ants, and their jaws are as sharp as a pair of scissors. When the piece is nearly cut through, the ant gives it a jerk, and pulls it quite off. Often there will be a heap of leaves on the ground. The ant has dropped them. But some more ants come and carry them away.

The path, where the ants keep going backwards and forwards, gets as smooth and hard as if the wheel of a waggon had made it.

Besides stripping the trees, the ants are sad robbers in-doors.

They creep into the houses at night, and carry off what they can.

The people in Brazil eat meal made, as I told you, of mandioc root. The ants will come in the night, and make their way to a basket of meal.

They will carry it away, grain by grain, till the next morning it will all be gone.

A traveller in that country could not believe what the Indians said, about the ants doing so much mischief. But one night he had a proof of it. His servant woke him to tell him that rats must be in the baskets of meal, and would carry it all away.

He got up, and looked about for rats. But he soon found that the robbers were ants.

An army of ants were marching between the door and the table, where the baskets stood.

Part of the ants were going out, and part were coming in. The ants that were going out had each a grain of meal in its mouth, hurrying off with it.

The baskets were lined with leaves, and some of the ants were busy cutting pieces out of them, to carry away as well.

This made the rustling noise that had sounded like rats.

Of course the Indians, and the white people too, kill as many ants as they can. But if the ants have made an attack on any kind of food, it is no easy matter to get rid of them.

Fresh ants keep pouring in, to take the places of those who are killed, till the work of killing seems hopeless.

The best way is to put a train of gunpowder on their path, and then blow them up.

This great ant is called the Sauba Ant. It lives only in the hottest parts of America.

THE HANGING NESTS.

THE little birds that live in the forest have a great many enemies. The monkey likes to peep into their nest, and see if there is anything in it he can run away with. He is as fond of eggs as we are.

Then there comes the snake, winding slowly up the tree. If the poor mother bird sees him, she is in great distress. She flies round and round his head, making a screaming noise, as if she hoped to drive him away. But the snake takes no notice. His bright eye is fixed upon her. If she does not mind, she will flutter too near. He will open his great jaws and eat her up.

HANGING NESTS.

What is the little bird to do with such deadly enemies around her?

Nature tells her what to do. It teaches her to build her nest in as safe a place as she can find; and to make it in such a way that neither snake nor monkey can get in.

The nest in the picture is a little like a pouch or pocket. It hangs from the tree over a stream or river. It has an opening at the bottom, and the little bird is just going to fly in. She will fly up a dark narrow passage to the place where you see the pouch bulge out. Here the nest really is; and here she can sit upon her eggs, without any fear of the snake or of the monkey.

No creature, that has not wings to fly as she does, can come in.

What is the nest made of? It is made of woven grass, and is so strong, you would have hard work to pull it to pieces. The nest is dark; but what do you think the little bird has been known to do?

She has been known to catch the fire-flies, and stick them on the walls of the nest. She sticks them in bits of wet clay. The fire-flies shine like tiny lamps. Can she have put them there to light up her nest?

The bird that catches the fire-fly lives in Africa. Where does the bird in the picture live?

In South America. Travellers, in that country, see hundreds of hanging nests in the forest, or along the banks of the rivers.

INDIA-RUBBER.

I am going to tell you of another very useful tree, that grows in South America.

This tree has a sap which makes India-rubber.

It has a Latin name, but people call it the India-rubber tree.

It grows near a great river called the River Amazon.

The Amazon is the largest river in the world. If you look at the map you will see what a long way it flows. It flows on, and on, for two thousand miles.

One of the rivers that run into the Amazon has some low damp islands in the middle of the stream. In the rainy season the islands are covered with water. But when fine weather comes again, they get dry, and people can go upon them.

Great forests grow over the islands; and here it is, that the India-rubber trees are found.

People come every year to get the sap.

Getting the sap is called tapping the tree.

A man will have a certain number of trees to tap. He goes round in the evening, and makes great cuts in the bark of the trees.

Wherever he cuts the bark, a milky juice trickles out. It runs into a little clay cup, or a shell, that is put under the wound to receive it.

THE INDIA-RUBBER TREE.

The man goes away, and leaves the sap to trickle. But the next morning he comes again. The clay vessel will be full of sap, and he dips a mould into it. He goes on dipping it, till the mould has two or three coats of sap. Of course, he lets one coat dry before he puts on the next.

The sap that sticks to the mould is white and hard. But the man makes a fire of palm-nuts. A thick black smoke rises from the burning nuts, and he passes the mould through it again and again. This gives the hardened sap a dark colour.

The sap is now India-rubber, and is ready to be sold.

In this country we have so many things made of India-rubber, that if I were to name them all it would be a very long list indeed.

Bags, and caps, and over-shoes, and coats, and cloaks, are all made of it. Besides tents, and boats, and even bridges. Not a drop of water can find its way through India-rubber, so you may think how valuable it is!

THE EEL THAT GIVES A SHOCK.

NATURE gives to every creature the means of defending itself from its enemies.

Some creatures are very strong; some can run very fast; some have a shell or shield on their bodies, like the turtle.

But there is one fish that has a very curious way of defending itself.

ELECTRIC EEL.

It can give shocks like an electric machine.

People call it the electric eel.

When it is angry, it can give such a great shock that a man would be knocked down by it.

Where does the electric eel live?

In South America. It swims about in the great rivers, such as the Amazon and the Orinoco.

THE EEL THAT GIVES A SHOCK.

HUNTING THE EELS.

When an Indian goes to bathe, he often gets a shock from an eel.

He cannot very well catch the eel in these great rivers, though he often tries.

He throws the root of a plant into the water. If the eel comes and nibbles at the root, it gets stupid and as if it were tipsy. Then sometimes the Indian contrives to catch and kill it.

But in the pools and smaller streams it is easy to kill a great many eels.

Some of the pools in the Llanos are full of eels, and they kill all the fish. They give the poor fishes a shock, and then eat them.

The Indians come with a number of mules and horses when they want to hunt the eels.

They are rather cruel to the poor horses. They drive them headlong into the pool in order that the eels may tire themselves out by giving them shocks.

When the eels are tired out, they will be safer to meddle with.

The poor horses do not like going into the pool. The eels swim under their bodies, and begin to give them shock after shock.

You see what distress the horses are in. They splash about as if they were mad. Their manes stand up and their eyes roll, and they pant and snort, and make all kinds of noises. They would get out of the pool if the Indians would let them. But every time they try, the Indians drive them back.

What with the shouts and cries of the Indians, the splashing of the water, and the fury of the horses, it is a very wild scene indeed.

After a time the eels get tired, and their shocks grow less and less. The horses become less furious, and do not splash about so much. The eels have used up their electricity, and they will want rest and food to get a fresh supply.

It is now safe for the Indians to come near them, and they begin to throw their spears, or harpoons.

The eels have come to the edge of the water, where it is easy to spear them.

But now and then, an eel is speared before its power of giving shocks has come to an end.

If an Indian ventures to touch it, the eel would give such a shock that he would fall backwards and be quite stunned.

A NARROW ESCAPE.

One day, some men went down the River Amazon in a boat.

The river ran through one of the great forests, and there were many things for the men to look at. Long-legged birds, with bright scarlet feathers, stood on the bank looking out for fish.

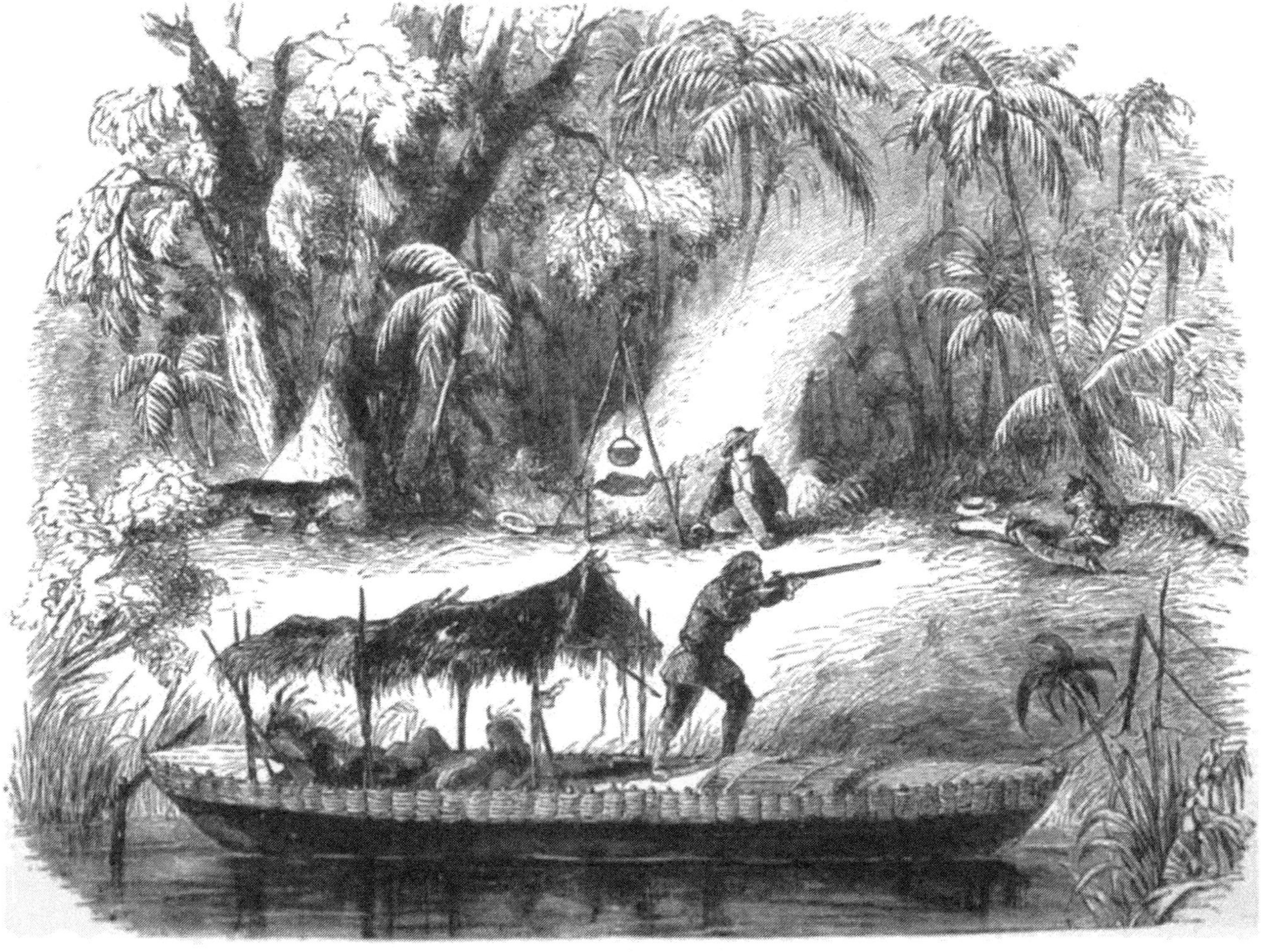

A NARROW ESCAPE.

They were called flamingoes.

Monkeys ran about on the long twisted cables that went from one tree to another, and kept up a constant chatter. Bright-coloured parrots climbed about the branches; and here and there, the humming-bird flashed among the deep-green leaves.

The men were never tired of looking about them.

But dinner-time came, and they began to be hungry. Then they pushed the boat ashore, and went on land to cook their dinner.

What was their dinner?

A wild hog. There are a great many in the forest, and they are very good to eat. These men had killed one on purpose.

You see how they are cooking it. They have run a spit through it, and have hung it over the fire. When it is done, it will be very nice indeed.

The men were rather tired with their journey. One man lay down on the ground and went fast asleep. His friends were busy turning the meat round and round, for fear it should burn. The roast meat soon began to smell very savoury. The men thought what a good dinner they should have.

The forest was very thick with shrubs and bushes. All among these bushes a fierce wild beast was lurking.

I mean the jaguar.

The jaguar was near enough to smell the roast meat, and he came crouching on, with his body close to the ground. He came nearer and nearer. No one saw him. The two men who were cooking had their backs to him.

He came close up to the man who was asleep on the ground. Then he stopped.

Did he spring on the man?

No; perhaps he was not very hungry. He lay down, and began to pat the man's feet with his paw.

Did he waken the man?

No; the man was as sound asleep as ever. What dreadful danger he was in! All at once, the other men turned round. You may think how they started at the sight. There was not a moment to lose.

You see one of the men has snatched his gun. He is going to shoot the jaguar through the head.

People dare not go a step in these forests without a gun.

When the gun went off, the man awoke. He was in no danger now, for the jaguar was dead.

How thankful he must have felt to have been saved from a cruel death!

DIAMOND WASHING.

DIAMOND WASHING.

WHAT are the black men in the picture doing?

They are hunting for diamonds.

Once the negroes, who were looking for gold, found little bright stones among the sand and gravel.

At first, they threw the stones away. But a man picked them up, who knew more about the little bright stones than the negroes did. He knew they were diamonds.

What a rich country that must be! To have both gold and diamonds!

The country is Brazil.

The black men in the picture are close to a river. The water is made to run through the troughs they are working in. It goes in at one end, and out at the other. The trough is full of mud and sand, taken from the river. The water, as it runs through, keeps washing the mud, and the negroes keep raking it. They hope to find diamonds.

Do they find any diamonds?

Sometimes a negro finds one, and then he claps his hands. The men that you see sitting on chairs, and looking on, are overseers. They sit there to make the negroes work, and to prevent them from stealing the diamonds. When a negro has found a diamond, he takes it between his finger and thumb, and gives it to the overseer. The overseer puts it into a bowl of water. By the end of the day, he has a great many diamonds in his bowl.

Do you see that negro holding up his hands? He is very glad indeed. He knows he shall be free. He has found a large diamond. One that weighs a great deal more than the rest.

THE INDIAN'S MEDICINE.

THERE is a very sad complaint called the ague.

When a man has the ague, he shivers with cold, and his teeth chatter in his head.

Then he begins to burn with fever, and so he is cold and hot by turns.

What gives people the ague?

Living in a place where the ground has not been drained.

The Indians who live in the forests of Peru are very apt to have the ague. But a tree grows in Peru that can cure them.

It was not known for a long time what a useful tree this was.

But one day, a poor Indian, who had the ague, stooped to drink of a pool in the forest.

The water was very bitter, but the Indian was hot with fever, and he drank a great deal of it.

What made the water bitter?

THE INDIAN'S MEDICINE.

GATHERING PERUVIAN BARK.

Some trees had fallen into it. And the bark of the trees had made it bitter.

After the Indian had drank, he began to feel better, and was soon quite well. He told the other Indians what had cured him. And it began to be known that the bark of the tree was as good as medicine.

What is the name of the tree? It is called Cinchona, after a lady who had the ague.

The lady was a countess, and she was cured by drinking of the pool of bitter water in the forest.

In England, we call the medicine Peruvian bark.

How do people get the bark?

Some men go into the forests to look for the Cinchona trees.

The men have a master over them, who has a hut, and even sows a little corn round it.

He does not know how long he and his men will have to be in the forest.

Then the men go different ways, each looking for the trees.

The forest is so thick that each man has to carry a hatchet, and keep chopping as he goes. He keeps all the time a very

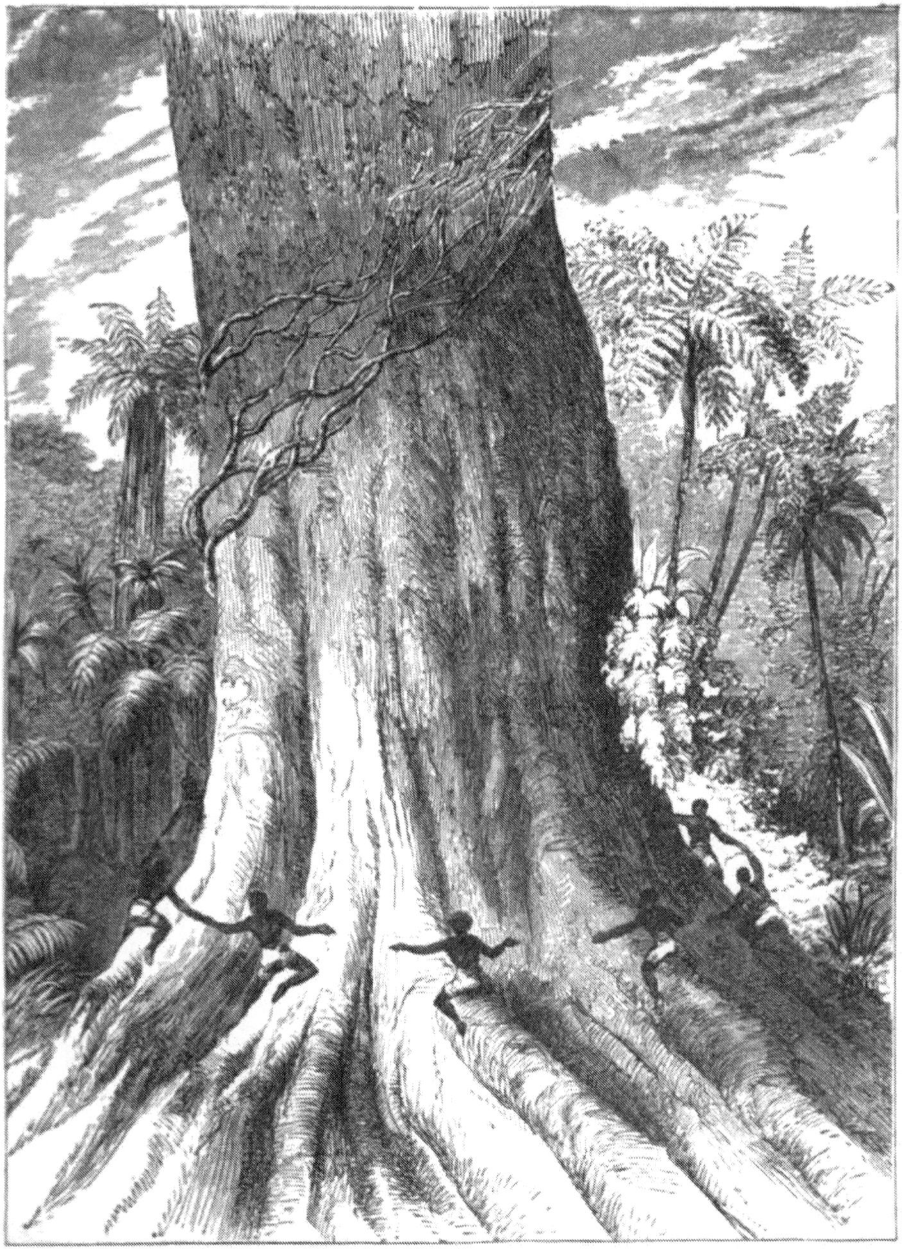

A GIANT TRUNK.

sharp look out. If he spies any dry leaves on the ground, he will know in a minute, whether they came from the tree he wants.

Then he will take notice which way the wind is blowing. And he will go in that direction.

Sometimes he may go on, day after day, without coming to the tree. And sometimes he will get lost amongst the great trunks and bushes, and never be heard of again. So that getting Peruvian bark is no very easy matter.

When the tree is found, the men set to work to cut it down.

But when the trunk is cut through, it will still stand upright. Those long streamers, called vegetable cables, are so twisted about it that they hold it up. They are round the other trees as well, and will not let it fall. These have all to be cut through before the tree can be set at liberty. Then the bark is taken off the trunk. You may see it in the shops in England.

THE GIANT TRUNKS.

In some of the forests of Brazil it is scarcely possible to get along at all.

Not only the vegetable cables block up the way, but shrubs grow so thick between the trees that they fill up every atom of space. In the deep recesses of the forest, it is very hot indeed. No air can get between the matted boughs. After the great floods that happen during the wet season, the damp mist hangs in wreaths on the tops of the trees.

In the heat of the day there is a deep silence in the forest. The wild beasts lie down in their dens. The birds creep into their nests. Now and then a crash is heard, as of a falling tree; or there will be a wild cry, as of some creature being pounced upon and devoured.

Then all will be silent again.

At sunset the creatures wake up. The wild beasts prowl about. There are frightful noises, and growls, and shrieks, and roars.

The forest is all alive, and its inhabitants are preying one upon the other.

In these mighty forests the soil is as rich as can be. There will be layer upon layer of rich black mould, made by the succession of trees and plants that have gone to decay.

For ages have these trees gone on growing, coming to perfection, and then decaying.

Your life or mine would be as a speck of time compared to theirs!

Do you see that giant tree in the picture?

People think it has been growing for more than two thousand years. What a space it is round! Fifteen Indians, with their arms stretched out, can but just reach round it. A man can easily get lost behind such trees as these.

If he shouted at the pitch of his voice, his companions could not hear him; and he might wander about till he died.

THE INDIAN'S BLOW-PIPE.

THE Indian has not many tools to work with. But he contrives to make a very ingenious weapon, that he can shoot arrows from, as well as from his great bow.

This weapon is called a blow-pipe.

In the picture you will see what it looks like. It is a very long tube, and is made of two hollow pieces of wood, which are strapped together very tightly. The strap is made of the wood of the climbing palm. Then the tube or blow-pipe is smeared over with wax.

It has a mouth-piece for the Indian to blow through, and is so heavy that he cannot carry it, unless he is a full-grown man.

The Indian lads use a little blow-pipe to practise on.

The arrows are not large, but they are very sharp, and are tipped with poison.

They are blown out of the tube by the breath of the Indian, and make a noise as they go off, like a pop-gun.

HUNTING WITH THE BLOW PIPE.

The Indian holds his blow-pipe quite steady, and takes aim a long way off.

The arrow goes winging its way, and scarcely ever misses. It is better in some respects than a gun.

The flock of monkeys or parrots would take fright if they heard a gun go off. But they do not hear the arrow, and one by one, they drop down wounded or killed.

Very soon, the hunter will have a heap of game by his side.

The white man cannot use the blow-pipe so well as the Indian.

He does not hold it so steadily, and is not so expert. I hardly think he could scoop out the blow-pipe with the only tool the Indian has to use.

What is the Indian's tool?

The sharp tooth of an animal.

THE GIANT WATER-LILY.

You have seen the large round leaves of the water-lily, lying on the surface of some stream or river, in our own pleasant land.

But do you know where the giant water-lily comes from?

I call it giant, because it is so much larger than any other water-lily, either in England or elsewhere.

VICTORIA REGIA.

It lives in the shallow lakes and pools made by the river Amazon.

THE GIANT WATER-LILY.

Its leaves are eighteen feet round, and the large white flowers lift themselves out of the water.

The leaf is so strong that a child might stand on it without getting into the water.

There is a bird which is often found standing on the leaf. It has long slender toes, and steps about over the lake, walking on the leaves.

Its home is in the woods and marshes near the river, and its name is Jacana.

Towards night the petals of the giant water-lily begin to unfold. At first they are pure white. Then they get rose-coloured, and end with being a deep red.

They scent the air with a delicious fragrance. But when three days are over, the flower fades and goes under water to ripen its seeds. The Indian gets the seeds, and roasts them for food.

Some years ago, a traveller was going along the banks of the river, when he came upon a lake quite hidden in the forest.

The lake was full of the giant water-lily, all spread out in its beauty.

He was so delighted that he wanted to jump into the water, and get some flowers. But the Indians held him back, and pointed to something which looked like a great log on the water.

It was an alligator that was lazily basking in the sun. If the traveller had gone near it, he might have been drawn under water and devoured.

He went on to the next town as fast as he could, and hired a canoe.

The canoe was launched on the lake, and then he began to get the leaf and flower of this wonderful plant. The leaves were so large that the canoe would only hold two of them.

The traveller brought the seeds of the giant water-lily to England.

He sent some of them to the Gardens at Kew, where all kinds of foreign plants are to be seen.

Did they grow?

Yes. They were set in a hot-house, in a tank of water. Here they grew well, and bore beautiful flowers.

The flower is called Victoria Regia, after her Majesty the Queen.

THE BABY'S BATH.

WHAT a famous bath this little baby is having!

Can you guess what the bath is made of?

It is not a tub, nor a basin, nor anything that you have ever seen.

The baby's mother did not buy it. She got it out of the forest. She uses it for many other purposes besides washing her baby in.

It is the spathe of the palm-tree.

What is the spathe?

The spathe is a great horny sheath that wraps up the buds before they come into flower. When the flowers are ready, they burst the sheath and open their petals.

Sometimes the spathe stands up, and sometimes it hangs down and glistens in the sun. At last it drops off, and the negro woman has picked it up from the ground.

It is very large, as you see in the picture.

What else comes from the palm-tree?

A great many more things than I can tell you about. Food, and wine, and clothing, and furniture, and houses, all come from the palm.

The banks of the rivers in Brazil are lined with a palm called the wax-palm.

How do people get the wax?

From the young leaves. The Indians cut them down, and let them dry in the sun. As they are drying, a number of scales will fall from their surface. When these scales are melted, they become white wax. The wax has to get cold, and then it is hard, and may be used.

People make candles of it.

The Indians get a constant supply of food from the wax-palm.

It bears a black shining fruit about the size of an egg. The Indian boils the fruit a long time, and then eats it with milk.

The young stems of the palm are full of soft pith, that is very white and good to eat. When he wants food, the Indian has only to cut down the palm-tree and take out the pith.

THE LAND OF THE GIANTS.

IF you look at the extreme south of the great continent of America, you will see a country called Patagonia. It is a bleak, dreary country. You see nothing but great plains, one a little above the other.

Grass grows on the plains, though it is coarse and wiry; and there are some valleys where grass grows as well. And there are bushes and shrubs. But no trees of any size grow in Patagonia.

The climate is very cold. In winter a cutting wind sweeps over the plains. There is a short, hot summer, when all the grass is dried up.

Very little rain falls, and there are not many streams of water. A few springs and pools are found in the valleys, but the water has an unpleasant taste. Still, the natives are obliged to drink it.

Who are the natives?

THE LAND OF THE GIANTS.

YOUNG PATAGONIANS.

A race of savage Indians. They are so tall, they look almost like giants. They wear mantles of skins sewed together. The skins are taken from an animal a little like the llama, and which lives in Patagonia. This animal is very swift-footed, and roams about in herds.

It is called the guanaco.

The Indian clothes himself with its skin, and he eats its flesh. In fact, it is one of the few comforts he has.

He is a frightful-looking Indian. He has thick, coarse hair, which hangs over his shoulders. He has a large head, and high cheek-bones. His face, and indeed his skin is painted all over, and he paints white circles round his eyes.

THE CASSOWAY.

He lives in a hut or tent made of skins, and open on one side.

His tent is bare and empty. There is nothing in it but a few skins for his bed, and the weapons that he hunts and fights with.

He has a sharp knife like a dagger, and he has the bolas.

What is the bolas?

It is a strap of leather, ten or twelve feet long, which he uses as a sling.

He has two great stones, or balls, if he can get them. He fixes one of the balls in his sling, and whirls it round and round his head. All this time he is on horseback, galloping as fast as he can. When the stone has got great force with being whirled, he flings it at the animal he means to kill. Both sling and stone go flying through the air together. The stone knocks the poor animal down, and often kills it at once. If it is not killed, the leather sling winds round and round it, and prevents it from getting away.

The Indian hunts the guanaco with the bolas. Often a troop of Indians go out on horseback, and attack a whole herd. Then there is a grand whizzing of the bolas through the air, until a great many of the guanaco are killed.

The better an Indian can hunt, the more honour he gets from his tribe.

Very often he will hunt the cassoway.

What is the cassoway?

It is a long-legged bird like the ostrich, only smaller. It runs over the plain so swiftly, that the horse cannot always overtake it.

Its flesh is tender, and good to eat.

The Indian thinks a great deal of the cassoway.

He has plenty of horses, and rides about everywhere. He steals them when he can from neighbouring countries. Horse-stealing is quite a trade in Patagonia.

The more horses an Indian can steal, the better he is thought of.

THE SAND STORM.

You have heard of the Prairie and the Pampas. I am going to tell you, now, something about the Llanos.

The Llanos are in South America. They stretch from the mountains on one side, to the sea-coast on the other. To the mouth of the great river Orinoco.

Thousands of square miles are enclosed within the limits of the llanos!

THE SAND STORM.

A SAND STORM.

What an immense, far-stretching plain it is!

This tract of country is near to the Equator. But it is not like the great Desert of Sahara. Oh no! Every year, floods of rain descend upon it, and then it has a coating of green grass.

In the hot weather, the grass is dried up with the heat. Day after day the sun beats down upon it. Every pool and spring is dried up. Then there often happens what you see in the picture.

What is it in the picture?

It looks like a water-spout. But it is not water. It is sand.

When a sand storm is coming on, the ground trembles, as if there were going to be an earthquake. It gets dark, for clouds of sand rise up and fill the air. The wind seems to blow from all quarters at once. The currents of air pushing against each other make the sand rise up like a column or spout. The column moves on, and seems as if it would overwhelm whatever came in its path.

See how the poor animals are running to get out of its way! But the storm will soon be over, and the sun will shine as brightly and as fiercely as ever.

THE LIGHTS' IN THE TREES.

Who lives in the Llanos?

A great many people. Here and there are villages. But there are vast plains and deserts without any people living in them at all.

White men live in the villages, and keep cattle. There are hundreds and thousands of cattle in the llanos. The Indian lives there too. He likes to live near the fan-palm. The fan-palm grows by the mouth of the river Orinoco.

He belongs to a tribe that are very poor indeed. He is very wild and ignorant. He would be half starved if it were not for the fan-palm.

Why is it called the fan-palm?

Because its leaves spread out in the shape of a fan.

This whole tribe of Indians depend on the palm for their living.

The soft pith in the stem makes them a kind of meal. The sap is their wine. They have no fear of famine while they have the fan-palm.

Part of the year, the plain is under water.

What becomes of the Indians then? Have they boats to live in?

No. I will tell you what they do. They hang their huts in the trees. Their huts are very simple. They weave a mat of the stalks of the palm leaves. This makes the floor of the hut. They hang these mats up in the branches, and make a roof over them of clay. This is all. When they want to cook anything, they light a fire. The mat-floor is always damp, so there is no danger of setting their house on fire.

People sailing down the river, at night, see a row of lights in the trees. They know what it means. The Indians are cooking their suppers.

THE CROCODILE IN THE MUD.

What animals live in the Llanos? All the herds I told you about, of wild cattle, horses, and mules. And a great many fierce beasts.

The jaguar or American tiger; and the puma or American lion; and wherever there is a pond or stream, there is the crocodile.

In hot weather, the poor animals suffer very much indeed. The springs are all dried up, and there is nothing for them to drink. Even the pools, under the shade of the fan-palm, vanish by degrees.

Then, what can the poor animals do?

The crocodile buries himself in the mud at the edge of the pond, and gets as deep as he can. The horses gallop about with out-stretched necks. The mules are more cunning than the horses. They hunt about for a plant which grows in the plain, and is called the melon cactus.

The cactus is, as you know, very prickly outside; but the mule, with his hard hoof, stamps off the prickles. Then he puts his mouth to the fruit, and sucks it. The juice is very cool and pleasant. But it often happens, that one of the great prickles gets into the foot of the mule and lames him. When night comes, the air is cooler, but the poor cattle do not enjoy much peace. Out fly large bats, that hover over them.

The bats make no noise, except a soft humming sound. But they drop down on the horse or mule, and give him a little bite. The horse scarcely feels the bite; but for all that, the bat is sucking his blood.

At last the dry weather breaks up. The deep blue sky gets of a lighter colour. The stars shine with a less steady light. A few clouds get

THE CROCODILE IN THE MUD.

up, and spread themselves over the sky. Thunder mutters in the distance, and down comes the welcome rain.

All nature revives. The ground, lately so bare, is covered with soft green grass. Flowers spring up, and birds begin to sing.

The horses and mules can drink as much as they like. The pools are filled with water, and the mud by the edge of the ponds becomes soft. All at once, a strange noise is heard. Some travellers are, perhaps, sleeping in a hut. The floor of the hut moves, and something heaves itself slowly up. What can it be? It is the crocodile, that wants to come out and enjoy the rain.

A STRANGE VISITOR.

His great body rises up from the bed of mud. He stares about him, as if in wonder. Everybody gets out of his way, and when he has fairly freed himself, he sets off at a clumsy pace, and plunges into the pond.

PAMPAS.

I AM going to tell you about another great plain in South America. If you look on the map in the southern part of South America you will see a place called Buenos Ayres. Just below Buenos Ayres is the pampas.

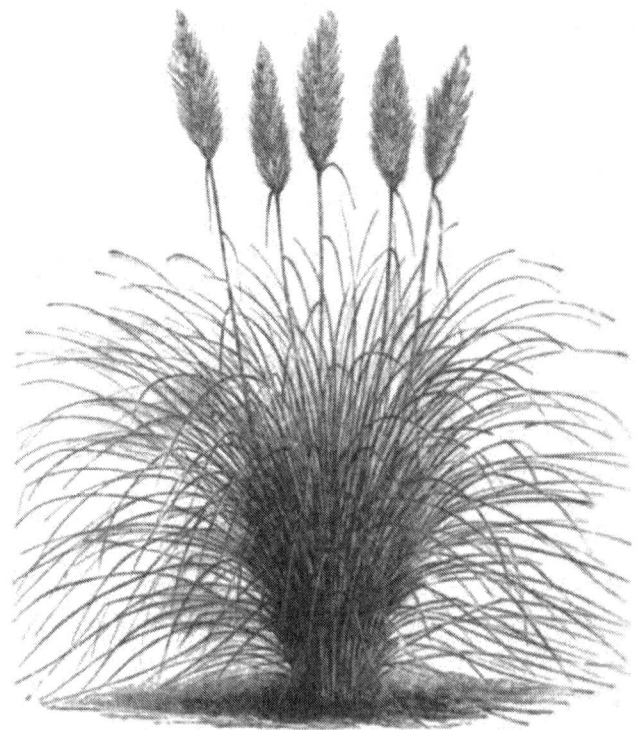

PAMPAS GRASS.

The first part of the pampas is covered with thistles and clover. In spring, before the clover comes up, the thistles have it all their own way. They grow up so tall and strong, and are so prickly, that not even an animal can push his way between them. There is quite a forest of thistles; but, after a time, they begin to fade; their bright flowers decay, their leaves shrivel up, and their stems are black and dead. The bare stems rattle against each other, until, at last, the weather changes. Down pours the rain; the wind howls across the plain, and the stems are beaten down to the ground. Then they soon rot, and are seen no more.

But up springs the clover, fresh and green and beautiful. The plain is soon covered over, and the animals come and feast at their leisure.

The next part of the pampas is covered with grass. When you have passed the thistles and the clover you come to a vast sea of rolling grass, which reaches for many miles. Then there is a kind of wood or forest, only that the trees do not grow close together. A man on horseback could gallop among them in all directions.

What with trees, and grass, and clover, the pampas is a very wonderful place!

The grass in the picture is called Pampas Grass. You see how beautiful it is.

People in England admire it very much, and plant it on their lawns, to look at. But it does not like frost, and has to be wrapped up in the winter.

The flower is feathery, like a reed, and of a silvery white colour.

There are miles and miles of this grass on the pampas. When the wind blows gently over it, the flowers glisten, and look a little like the spray of the sea when the sun is shining on it.

The wild horses gallop about as they do in the prairies, and other great plains in this part of the world. A race of people live here who are very fond of horses. When a child can scarcely toddle, he is thought old enough to get on horseback. His whole life will be spent on horseback. As he gets older, he will gallop after the wild horses and catch them with the lasso.

What is the lasso?

A strip of leather with a noose at one end of it.

Are the men Indians?

No; they are descended from the Spaniards. But they lead the lives of Indians. They do not rove about, because there is no need. They would never find so much beef anywhere as in the pampas, and they do not care to eat anything but beef.

How do they get beef?

There are vast herds of cattle in the pampas. When a man has come to the end of his beef, he has only to ride out, with his lasso in his hand, among the wild cattle. He can soon throw his lasso over the horns of one of them, and bring it to the ground. He has a sharp long knife in his hand, with which he kills it.

He does not care to grow corn or vegetables, or to build houses and plant gardens.

As long as he can get enough beef, and ride about all day, he does not mind.

His house is a mere hut made of mud. The poorest man in England would hardly like to live in such a place. He thatches his hut with grass; and what do you think he uses instead of chairs? Seats made of horses' heads!

The baby is slung in a cradle of bullock's skin, that hangs from the roof.

These half-savage men are called Guachos. They wear a short cloak made of leather; and very wild they look as they gallop about, their black hair streaming in the wind.

There are Indians in the pampas who are yet more savage. They ride about on horseback, and ride faster than the white men. And they often rob the poor hut, and set it on fire. Then the whole family will perhaps be murdered.

CROSSING THE ANDES.

THE great mountains of the Andes are in South America. Their peaks are covered with snow. They are the grandest mountains in the world. See how many miles they reach, all down the western coast of South America!

Can people travel over them?

They do sometimes. But you see how dangerous it is. If they were to fall over the edge, they would be killed in a moment. There is a narrow ledge for a road—so narrow there is but just room for the feet. If you looked down, you would see a deep chasm—so deep it makes you tremble to think of. It is better to look straight forward, or even to shut your eyes.

An Indian goes as a guide. He has been over these places a great many times, and his head does not grow dizzy. But even he has hard work to keep from falling. He has caught hold of the branch of a tree; that helps him on a little.

People always ride on mules. A man who was not used to the mountains would be sure to slip and stumble. And then he would roll over the edge, and no one could save him. It is far better to go on a mule. The mule does not slip. He is very careful where he sets his feet. He knows the way, and does not want guiding. The man on his back has only to sit quite still, and let the mule alone. He will get to the end of the dangerous place in safety.

CROSSING THE ANDES.

If he were to pull at the bridle, the mule might give a start, and then man and mule would both be over the chasm.

Sometimes the mule comes to a rock as steep as a house-side.

How does he go down it?

He does not attempt to walk. He knows he cannot. He draws his feet close together, all four of them, and slides down from the top to the bottom.

I should not much like to travel on the Andes!

THE HIGHEST VOLCANO IN THE WORLD.

MANY of the high peaks of the Andes are volcanoes.

One of these is the highest volcano in the world. It has rather a hard name.

It is called Cotopaxi.

This great mountain towers up to the sky. It has a smooth cone, and when it is going to have an eruption the snow that lies on the cone begins to melt.

Then the cone looks red and gloomy, and the rest of the mountain is of an awful blackness.

You may think what a grand sight it must be!

The melted snow that runs down the mountain makes a flood.

It sinks into the holes and caverns of the mountain. There it makes pools and rivulets.

After the mountain has become quiet, these hidden streams go on getting larger. The mountain torrents drip into them, and swell them, and fishes begin to swim about. For fishes like these hidden places, where they are out of the way of their enemies.

For some years the pools will go on getting larger, and more and more fishes will swim about in them.

But suddenly the mountain will begin to tremble. An earthquake always happens just before an eruption. The mountain shakes so violently that great cracks come in its side. Then out will pour a torrent of mud, and water, and fishes, and spread all over the country.

One little fish that had never been seen before, was thrown out in one of these eruptions.

COTOPAXI.

Once, so many fishes came out of a volcano, and spread themselves over the country, that for two miles nothing was to be seen but dead fishes and mud.

Of course, nothing could grow. The fields were made quite barren; and, what was worse, the smell of the dead fish brought on a fever.

THE COW TREE.

NEAR the great mountains of the Andes, there grows a solitary tree.

The rock is barren, and there is nothing green to look at. The tree has leaves like leather. It is very tall, but its roots scarcely do more than take hold of the rock on which it grows.

What use can it be?

Let us watch and see what happens. The sun is just rising, and people are going to their work.

A troop of white men and Indians are coming towards the tree. They carry large bowls made of the gourd, and they want some milk for their breakfasts.

Where is the milk to come from?

Not from the cow. There are no cows to be seen. The milk will come from the tree.

This is why it is called the Cow Tree.

How can milk come from a tree?

You must watch a little longer, and see what the men do. They make a hole in the bark with their hatchets, and out flows a white juice like milk. They soon fill their bowls. Some of them will sit down, and drink the milk off at once. Others will carry it home for their children.

But is it as nice as milk?

Yes. A famous traveller has told us so. His name was Humboldt. He drank the milk himself, and said it was very sweet and very wholesome.

Another traveller saw the Cow Tree growing in the forest. In the picture you see him holding his bowl, while an Indian makes a wound with a hatchet.

THE INDIAN'S BEAST OF BURDEN.

THE people who live in Peru have a very useful animal. It is a little like a camel, only that it is so much smaller. It is sometimes called the "small camel." But its right name is the llama. The llama does not live anywhere but in America. And Peru is the country where the llamas abound.

It can go a long time without drinking, and it does not want much to eat.

The Indian makes the llama carry his burdens for him, and be in the place of a horse or a camel.

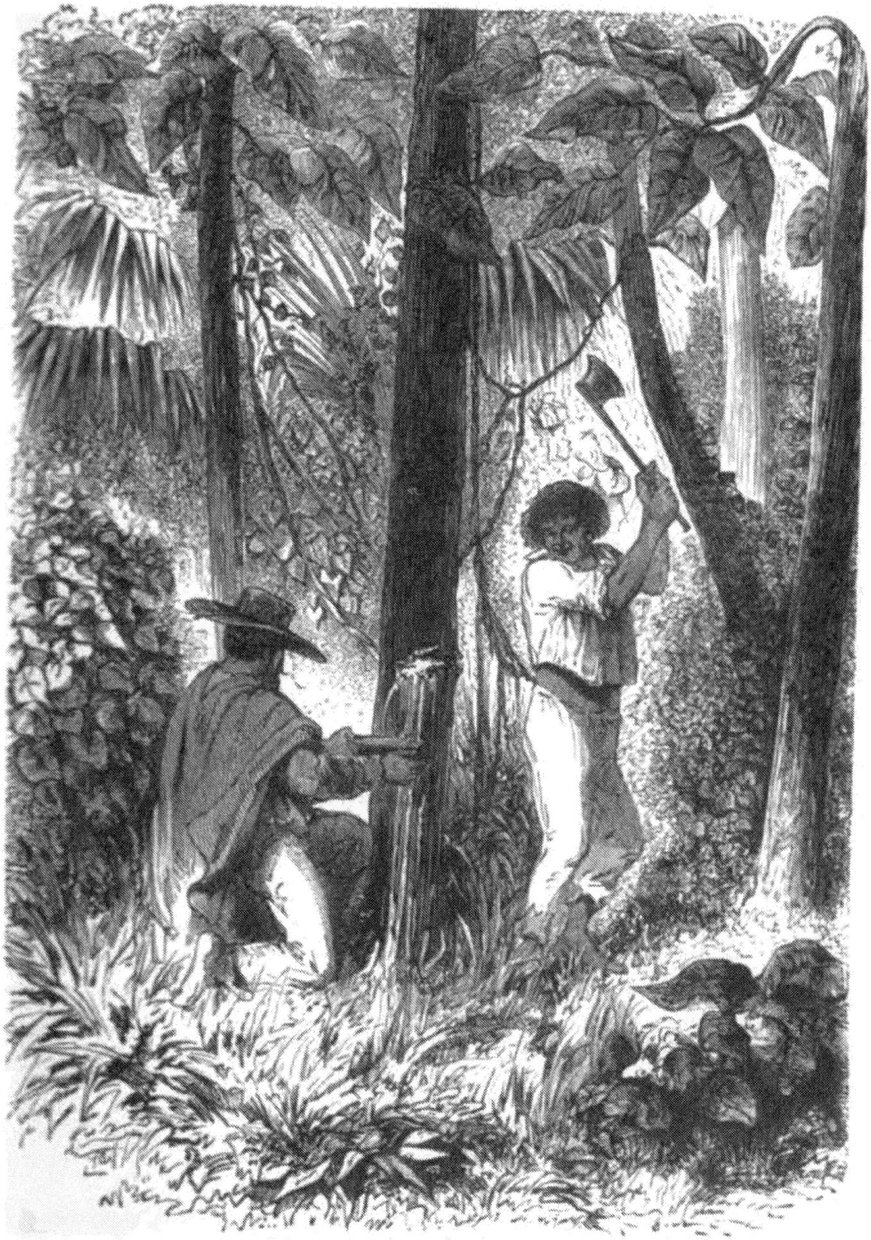

THE COW TREE.

THE INDIAN'S BEAST OF BURDEN.   149

It can go up and down the rocky places in the mountains without making a false step. The silver mines are up in the mountains; and the llama goes backwards and forwards, bringing loads of silver ore; a great many llamas will go, one after the other, in a file. They will have bows of ribbons on their heads, and bells round their necks.

LLAMAS.

Their masters are very fond of them, and like to see them look smart.

But if a llama gets too great a load put on its back, it will lie down; and nothing can make it get up until some of the load is taken off.

The wild llamas range about the mountains, and have a great deal more spirit than the tame ones.

They are as swift as the stag, and leap from rock to rock like the goat.

If any one comes in sight, off they scamper, and climb to the very tops of the mountains.

What mountains are they?

The great mountains of the Andes.

The llama has a nice woolly coat on its back. The Indian spins it into woollen cloth.

And a great deal of it comes to England, and is spun by our machines, and made into a stuff called llama.

Ladies have gowns made of it.

THE SHARK.

Of all the fishes that live in the sea, there is not one so savage or so much to be dreaded as the shark.

You see what a size he is! His mouth is so large, and his throat

THE SHARK.

so wide, that he can swallow a man with ease. His teeth are very sharp and very strong. There are six rows of them, and they lie flat in his mouth when he is not eating. But if any poor creature comes near him, up start all the teeth, and he darts at it and devours it.

He has great round eyes that he can turn about all ways, so that he can see on every side of him.

His skin is hard, and rough, and prickly. Still man can turn it to account.

When it has been polished, it makes a leather called shagreen, and is used for spectacle-cases, and such like articles.

The shark can swim so fast, that he can keep up with a ship if it is going ever so swiftly.

He likes to keep up with a ship, because then he can catch whatever is thrown overboard.

He is not at all dainty, as you will think, when I tell you a pair of old boots was one day thrown at him.

The shark swam up, opened his great jaws, and swallowed them as if he thought them very nice.

The worst of it is, that if a man fell into the sea he would have no chance for his life. The shark would dart at him, and swallow him down in a minute.

The sailors set to work to get rid of the shark. They know how greedy he is, and they put a piece of meat on a hook, and fasten it to a long chain.

Then they throw the hook into the sea, and watch what happens.

Very soon, the shark begins to smell the meat. He is not far off, and he comes swimming up to the hook.

He does not seem to like the chain, and he will swim round it, and go away, and come back again. Then the sailors give the chain a pull. The shark gets into a fright. He thinks the meat is going to be taken away. He comes swimming up again, and opens his great jaws and swallows down the piece of meat. The moment he has done this, it is all over with him.

THE SHARK.

The sailors pull him to the ship by the chain, and he cannot get away, let him struggle as much as he will.

Very soon he is killed, and then there is an end of him.

THE SHARK IS CAUGHT AT LAST.

The shark lives in all parts of the world.

Some large lazy sharks come even to the British shores. They are quite harmless, and lie basking on the top of the water. This is why people call them "basking sharks."

It is when the shark lives in the Torrid Zone that he is so fierce and savage.

THE TYPHOON, OR GREAT WIND.

Accidents are always happening.

If a man bathes in the sea, he is in danger of having his arms, or his legs, snapped off by the great teeth of the shark.

THE TYPHOON, OR GREAT WIND.

The men in the picture are Chinese, and they set out one fine morning to catch fish. While they were busy fishing, the wind changed, and began to blow in great gusts. The sea tossed about in great waves, and looked wild and stormy.

The fishermen knew what was going to happen. They knew that the Typhoon was coming as fast as it could.

What is the typhoon?

It is a great wind that blows at certain seasons of the year. It lifts up the waves, and makes them run mountains high. Ships are driven about as if they were feathers.

When the fishermen saw the gale coming on, they pulled in their nets as quickly as they could, and tried to get home.

But I am afraid they are too late, and that most of their boats will be upset.

Do you see the city in the distance?

The moment the weather began to change, people ran about the streets, crying out that the great wind was coming.

Then all hands were at work.

The mats that hung before the doors and windows, to keep out the sun, were taken down. Props were put against some of the houses that were old and creaky, to prevent them from being blown away.

The farmers ran into the fields, and cut all the grain they could, and brought it home. The ripe fruit was plucked, all in a minute, and brought under shelter. Both the grain and the fruit would have been blown into the river.

When they have done all they can, the people run into their houses, and shut the doors and windows.

Very soon comes the great wind.

It comes howling, and tearing, and sweeping everything before it. Each gust seems more dreadful than the last.

The dust and the mortar come rattling down from the ceiling. The chairs and tables are covered with it.

Out of doors, you could not stand. The wind would blow you off your feet. The river rises, and swells, and overflows its banks. The whole country is like a lake.

The ships and boats, that have been fastened out of reach of the wind, are as safe as they can be. But often the fury of the gale breaks the chains that hold them. They will be floated out, and tossed to and fro at the mercy of the waves.

For a day and a night this great wind goes on blowing. Then it abates, and people can venture out of their houses.

But what a scene meets their eyes! The streets are full of rubbish and broken tiles. Many of the houses have been blown down. The gardens have lost all their beauty. Flowers and fruits have been stripped off. The crops which have been left in the field are ruined. Trees have been torn up by the roots.

What a dreadful thing is the typhoon!

THE TEA-FARMER.

ONCE upon a time, there was no tea at all in England.

People used to drink ale, and a sweet kind of wine called mead.

Great tankards of ale stood on the breakfast-table. Now we have tea and coffee.

Everybody likes tea in these days. When people are very tired, a cup of tea refreshes them as much as anything. When tea was first brought to

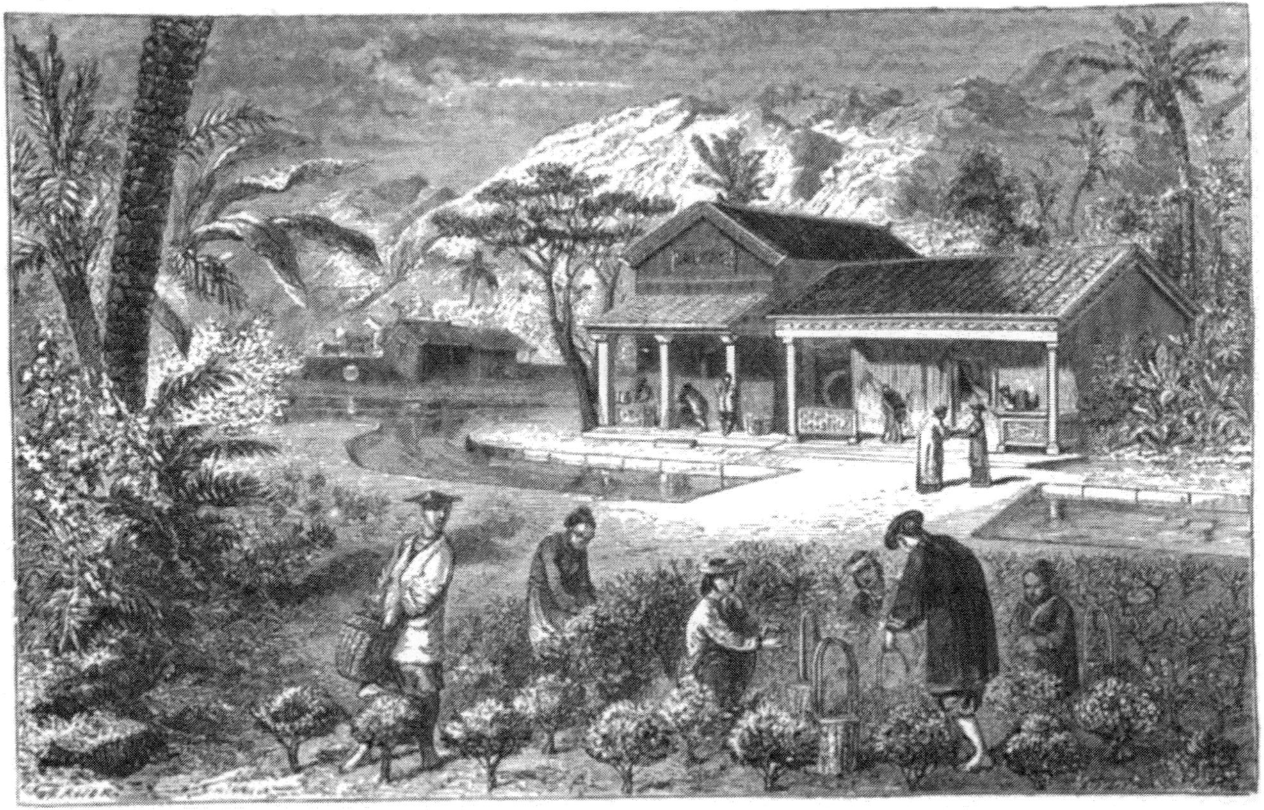

A TEA-FARM.

THE TEA-FARMER.

England, an old man and woman bought some as a great treat. But when they had it, they did not know how it ought to be made. They thought of a great many ways; at length they boiled the leaves, and strewed them on a piece of bacon they were going to have for dinner. So they ate the leaves, and threw the tea away.

In those days, a pound of tea cost a great deal of money. People drank it out of tiny cups that had no handles. You may have seen some of these little cups put upon the mantle-piece, and kept to look at.

How do the Chinese drink their tea?

Without either milk or sugar.

The minute a visitor comes into a house, the servant brings him a cup of tea.

Where does the tea come from?

It comes from China. It grows upon a shrub. The leaves of the plant make the tea.

Every cottager in China has his little tea-garden. He sells what he does not use, and buys food and clothing for his family.

When a man has a large piece of ground, and grows a great many tea-shrubs, he is called a tea-farmer. When the tea-leaves are ready to be gathered, the farmer and his family are very busy. They pull off the leaves and throw them into baskets. When the baskets are full, they are carried to the barn.

THE TEA PLANT.

How is the tea prepared?

The leaves are dried in iron pans over the fire. While they are drying, men and women keep turning them about. As soon as they begin to crack, they are taken out and put upon a table. Then the people who are busy preparing them, roll them up in their hands, and press all the juice they can out of them.

The leaves are next put into the air to dry them still more. When this is done, they have to go into the pan again over the fire. Here they begin to curl and twist, and look as they do in the tea-caddy.

After a time they are quite dried enough, and then the farmer picks the leaves over, and gets them ready for market.

He may be seen marching off to the town, with his chest of tea slung over his shoulder on a pole made of bamboo. The tea merchants have come to the town, and he wants to sell them his tea.

The merchant looks at it, and if he thinks it good tea he buys it.

Then the farmer marches home again, with a string of coins slung over his shoulder.

That is the money he has been paid for his tea.

EATING BIRDS' NESTS.

THE earth has many treasures that man risks his life to get. There are pearls in the ocean, and there is gold in the mine, and coal deep in the pit where it would make your head giddy to look down.

Man risks his life every day to get something or other that Nature has put almost out of his reach.

But who would risk his life for a bird's nest?

In China, the rich people have a dainty dish, and it is made of birds' nests.

No matter how hard they are to get, the Chinaman must have them; and he does. They are sold in the market, and he buys them.

Where do the nests come from?

From an island called Java.

The coast of Java is very steep, and the cliffs have great holes or caves in them. The waves toss and roar about the caves, and numbers of birds fly in and out. You can hardly see them for the spray.

EATING BIRDS' NESTS

The bird has a long name; but as it belongs to the swallow tribe, I shall call it a swallow.

What are the birds doing in the caves?

Building their nests and feeding their young ones.

There seems no place for the nest to be built upon. But the bird has found one. She fastens it to the roof and sides of the cave.

These are the nests that the Chinaman likes to eat.

THE NESTS THAT ARE EATEN.

But the cave is in the steep cliff, with the sea raging at the bottom.

How can any one get at the nests?

The men are let down from the top of the cliff by a rope-ladder, till they reach the cave.

Just think of the danger! If the rope were to break, or the men turn giddy, they would be dashed to pieces in a moment!

When the men reach the cave, they find the floor covered, as it always is, with the sea. They have to cling to the rough stones that stick out of the sides of the cave, and get a footing as they can. When they have got to the roof, they fasten ropes round the stones from side to side of the cave, and make a kind of rough bridge. On this bridge, they have to stand while they pull down the nests.

What danger these poor men are in! One false step, and they would be lost. They are not Christians; but they dare not be let down the cliff, until they have offered up a prayer. They ask their gods to take care of them, and they place gifts on the tomb of the man who first found out the cave.

Why are the nests thought so good to eat?

Because they are made of a kind of sea-weed. The bird swallows the sea-weed, and then brings it up in her mouth, quite soft and like pulp. She adds layer to layer until she has built her nest large enough. If the nests are old, they are not thought worth taking.

What do the nests taste like?

They are like jelly, and have no taste. But the Chinese cook puts in so many spices, and other things, that he makes them very nice indeed.

The people of Japan know that the birds' nests are only made of sea-weed. They get the same sea-weed, and beat it soft, and boil it to a jelly. Then they make mock birds' nests, and bring them to the market to sell.

THE CHINAMAN'S KNIFE AND FORK.

If you were to dine with a Chinaman, you would have to use chopsticks.

What are chopsticks?

They are two round pieces of ivory, with sharp points. The Chinaman eats his dinner with them, instead of a knife and fork.

It is not easy to eat with chopsticks. A dish is set before you with bits of meat swimming in gravy. You are very hungry, and you try to pick up a piece of meat with your chopsticks. After a great deal of fishing and diving, you do it. The dainty morsel is half-way to your mouth: but the chopstick slips, and down it goes into the dish.

It has to be fished up again, and again it may drop. This may happen three or four times, and you begin to despair of getting any dinner.

Your friend the Chinaman is too polite to laugh. He is sorry for you, and comes to your help.

How does he help you?

By taking his own chopsticks, which have been going backwards and forwards from the dish to his mouth, and picking up the bit for you.

He raises it to your mouth, and you have to eat it. It is like eating with another person's knife and fork.

The Chinaman does not like any people but those who live in his own country. He will not laugh at his guest before his face, but he will make plenty of fun of him behind his back.

"Look at this red-haired man," he will say. "He does not even know how to get his food to his mouth!"

THE CHINAMAN'S DINNER.

WHAT does the Chinaman have for his dinner?

If he is a rich man, he will have a great many dishes, and his dinner will last for hours. But before the dinner begins, he will have tea.

The tea is not made in a teapot. A few leaves are put into each cup, and boiling water poured upon them.

This is how the Chinaman makes his tea, and he ought to know the best.

He will have baskets of fruit and beautiful nosegays set on his dinner-table; and he will have little saucers of preserved seeds, and sweetmeats of all kinds.

His meats will be cut up into small pieces that he can take hold of with his chopsticks. He will have fish, and poultry, and game, and more dishes than I can tell you about.

A gentleman went to a feast in China. He counted many hundred dishes, and had to sit at table six hours.

What a long time that was to be at his dinner!

What does the poor man have to eat?

He eats any thing he can get.

In the market, you might see cages with dogs and cats in them. The poor cats make a sad mewing, as if they knew what was going to happen. The dogs sit with their ears drooping and their heads hanging down. But in China both dogs and cats are eaten for food.

The rich man, now and then, will have a cat served up at his table; but he will not care to eat the poor man's dinner of fried mice or rats. There are strings of mice and rats ready dressed for cooking, carried about for sale as rabbits are with us.

The poor man is glad to carry some of them home for his dinner.

A cottager in England would starve on the food which keeps the poor man, in China, and all his family.

FISHING WITH A BIRD.

THE Chinese have more ways than one of catching fish. They eat so much fish, that it is a good thing to be expert at taking them.

A man will wade into a pond with a basket in his hand. When he is in the water, he raises his hands above his head, and brings them down with a great splash. His feet are in the mud at the bottom of the pond. The fishes are frightened at the splashing noise, and they dive into the mud to hide themselves. The man can feel them moving about his feet. The moment he feels a fish, down he goes under water. You see nothing of him for a few seconds. But up he comes, the fish in his hand. He pops it into his basket, and begins to splash again. Then comes another silly little fish, and his basket is soon full.

But how does he fish with a bird?

I will tell you. The bird is called a cormorant. The fisherman comes sailing down the river, and the birds are perched on the side of his boat.

Sometimes, he will have as many as a dozen birds to fish with.

When he comes to the right place, he stops and tells his birds to begin.

He has a way of speaking to them, so that they understand what he means. Then they drop into the water, and look about for the fish. As they are greedy by nature, their master ties a bit of string round their throats to prevent them from swallowing the fish when they have caught it. The moment a bird sees the fish, he pounces upon it. It is in his bill

CHINAMAN FISHING WITH HIS BIRDS.

and he rises with it to the surface of the water. His master calls to him, and he brings the fish and drops it in the boat. Then, off he sets, to catch another.

A man may get a great many fishes, in the course of the day, if his birds work well.

Sometimes a bird is lazy, and seems inclined to play about and enjoy himself. But the fisherman soon puts a stop to this. He has a long cane, and he gives a sharp blow to the water close by where the lazy bird is. This frightens him, and he begins to be as busy as a bee.

TREPANG.

THE sea-cucumber is a living creature a little the shape of a cucumber. It floats about in the sea, and its body is very soft, and has no bones in it. It belongs to a tribe of creatures called jelly-fishes, because when they are brought out of the water they look like jelly.

There is one kind of sea-cucumber that is eaten for food. It is called trepang.

In the Chinese markets you see great heaps of trepang to be sold. The Chinaman thinks it does his health good to eat trepang.

Where does the trepang come from?

From the coast of New Holland. It is not a pleasant part of the coast. Savages live there, who are as fierce almost as wild beasts. But that does not prevent boats from coming to fish for trepang.

The boats come from Malacca. The people of Malacca are called Malays. They are very clever at this kind of fishing. They want to sell the trepang to the Chinese.

They bring a few iron kettles with them on shore, and they build a little shed. Then they begin to fish.

When the sun is the hottest, in the very middle of the day, down they dive into the water. They can see the trepang crawling about at the bottom of the sea. It is just the colour of the ground it crawls on; but the eye of the diver is very sharp, and he sees it in a minute. He would not see it half so clearly, if the sun were not just over his head.

SEA-CUCUMBER.

The divers cannot stay many seconds under water; but they keep coming up, and going down again, till the boat is filled with trepang.

Then they set to work to get it ready for the market.

They fill their iron kettles with sea-water, and set them on the fire to boil. The trepang are thrown into the boiling water. Then they are cleaned, and steamed, and, lastly, dried in the sun. If it rains, they are dried under the shed.

How does trepang taste?

Some people say it tastes like lobster; others say that it tastes like a piece of leather.

LITTLE FEET.

When the Chinese lady was an infant in her cradle, her mother put a tight bandage on her feet. This was done to prevent them from growing. The poor little child, as she grew up, did not have the bandage taken off. She could not run about and play as English children do. She could only hobble on her poor lame feet.

What was this done for?

Because the Chinese think a lady ought to have a very tiny foot, no bigger than that of a baby. If a woman has feet as Nature made them, they are quite shocked. "Look at that woman!" they say; "she has feet large enough to walk upon!"

The Chinese lady never has to walk. She sits in her husband's beautiful garden, and her servants wait upon her, and bring her tea and sweetmeats, and all that she wants. If she goes out, she rides in a chair that is like a sedan-chair, and is carried by two men.

She lives very much shut up in the house and garden, for the Chinese do not like their wives to be looked at. She amuses herself with fancy work, and paints pictures, and has a little music, and sometimes writes verses. And so she contrives to pass away her time.

Do all the women in China make their feet small?

No. The poor woman has to get her living, and it would never do to hobble about. Her mother did not bandage her feet, so she can walk as well as you or I can. It is only the ladies who have the little feet.

A gentleman once saw a Chinese lady go into a passion. She scolded and raved, and tore her hair, as if she had been mad. And then she threw herself on the ground, and kicked up her little feet into the air.

You may think how absurd she looked. The gentleman was very much ashamed of her, but he could scarcely keep from laughing.

A CHINESE WEDDING.

I must tell you a little story about the Chinese lady.

As soon as she is old enough to be married, her father chooses a husband for her.

She is never allowed to see him herself. Her father carries on all the courtship for her.

And the Chinaman is never allowed to see her. He does not know what kind of a young lady she is.

At last the wedding-day arrives. The bride is dressed in very gay clothes, and put into a sedan-chair.

She is going, for the first time, to see her husband.

A crowd of people go with her, carrying lighted torches, though it may be the middle of the day.

Before the sedan, is a band of musicians, with fifes and drums. The sedan is locked, and an old servant carries the key.

No one may open it but the bridegroom.

As soon as the procession reaches the house, the sedan is put down at the door.

Then out comes the bridegroom. I should think he is very anxious to know what kind of a lady he has married.

He unlocks the door and looks in.

She has a veil over her face, but he lifts it up.

Perhaps she is not good-looking enough, and he does not think he shall like her.

What is to be done then?

He shuts the door in a hurry, and tells the bearers to take the lady home again.

He has to pay a sum of money, but he does not mind that.

If she has a pleasant face, and he likes her, there is no shutting of the door.

He asks her to come in. And the sedan-chair goes back empty. Then there is a grand feast, and the Chinaman is married.

RICE INSTEAD OF CORN.

THE Chinaman does not grow corn as we do. He eats rice instead. Rice is the staple food of the tropics, as bread is with us.

But the rice plants have to live in water. Their roots must always be kept wet.

So what can the Chinaman do?

He is so very industrious, and takes so much pains, that his rice crop is sure to answer.

He will cut terraces on the side of a hill, one above the other, and grow his rice upon them. The rice plants look as green as can be. He keeps them always flooded.

Where does the water come from?

From a stream close by. He has a machine, called a water-wheel, that forces the water up to the highest of the terraces. Then it flows down and waters all the rest.

In spring, the Chinese farmer is busy getting his fields ready for the rice-plants to be set.

It is very hard work, for the field has to be under water, and it is like ploughing in the mud. But he goes to work cheerfully for all that, and he and the buffalo, that he uses to draw his plough, sink in, and wallow in the mire together.

But the work is done at last, and the plants set in rows a few inches apart.

Then all that remains to be done, is to keep them well flooded with water.

When the rice begins to turn yellow, the farmer knows it is getting ripe. Then the water is turned off from the field.

The Chinaman seems to do as he likes with any little stream that comes into his power. He can make it go up hill, or down, or wind about, just as he wants it.

The farming business is very much thought of in China. The emperor himself, grand as he is, takes notice of it.

In the spring, when the plants are going to be put in, he shuts himself up for three days, and prays that there may be a good crop. And he will even go into the field and throw a handful of rice seed on the ground, and plough it in.

BASKETS OF FIRE.

It is often very cold in China. In the winter there will be ice on the river. How do the people keep themselves warm?

Not by nice blazing fires, as we do. They have no fire-places. In the middle of the day, even though it is winter, the sun will be hot. So they never think of a fire.

They wear very warm jackets, lined with sheepskin. In the morning, when it is cold and frosty, they will put on two or three jackets, one over the other.

By-and-by, they begin to feel rather too warm. The sun has come out, and the ice has all melted. So they are glad to throw off a jacket.

As it gets hotter, another jacket is pulled off. By the middle of the day, the Chinaman is lightly clothed; and if he goes out, he carries an umbrella to keep the sun off.

But as evening comes on, it gets cold and frosty again. Then, one by one, he puts on all his jackets. The ladies are often very cold. Then they bring out their stoves.

They are tiny brass stoves, shaped like a basket. The lid of the basket is grated, and the inside is full of burning charcoal. The lady carries her stove about with her, and lets it stand on the table, or the floor. Then she can warm her hands and her feet.

A nurse, who carries a child in her arms, will hold a little stove under its feet to keep them warm. But it is only in severe weather that the stoves are brought out.

A gentleman who was staying in China, for the winter, was very cold indeed. In the long dark evenings he could not sit snugly by the fire as we do. There was neither fire nor fire-place. The wind came whistling through the cracks in his window, and nearly blew his candle out.

THE TALLOW TREE.

CANDLES are, as you know, made of tallow, and tallow is made of fat.

But in China there is a kind of tallow which comes from a tree.

The tree is about the size of a cherry tree, and the leaves are of a red colour. The seeds grow in a pod, and when they are ripe the pod opens.

The seeds are full of oil, and this oil has to be squeezed out and made into tallow.

The time for getting the seeds is in the winter, just when the leaves have fallen off. The seeds are first steamed over a fire, and then beaten gently in a mortar. When they have been beaten enough, they are put into a sieve and sifted to get the tallow out. The tallow looks like oil, and is very thick and coarse. But it goes into a machine, and the thick coarse part is pressed out of it. It is now clear and white, and gets solid enough to make candles of.

But though it looks so good, it is apt to melt. So the candle-maker dips his candles in wax to make them stronger. The wax is red, or green, or yellow, or any colour he likes. The candles which are burned in the temples of the idols, are very large, and have golden letters upon them.

The wicks of the candles are made of a bit of dry wood covered with the pith of a rush. This burns as well as if the wick were made of cotton.

What becomes of the seed when the oil has been squeezed out? The Chinese never waste anything. They either burn it as fuel in their stoves, or else use it to manure their land.

How many useful trees are planted for us by nature! I am going to tell you of another, that the Chinaman would be very sorry to do without.

CHINAMAN BUSY IN A THICKET OF BAMBOO.

THE bamboo grows wild in China, as it does in many other places. But the Chinaman finds it such a useful tree, that he cultivates it as well.

The more bamboo he has the better.

What kind of a tree is the bamboo?

It is really a grass, and belongs to the same order as the grass you see in the field.

But in the Torrid Zone the grasses grow to an immense size.

The stem of the bamboo is like the trunk of a tree. But every now and then it has a knot or joint, such as you see in the stem of the grass. At the top of the stem is a plume of feathery leaves, as green as emerald.

The bamboo is a very beautiful tree, as well as a useful one.

Almost everything in China is made of bamboo, both on the land and on the water.

And the Chinaman makes his paper of bamboo.

He soaks the young shoots in water, and covers them up with lime. Then they are taken out, cut into shreds, and dried in the sun. After this, they are boiled and pounded till they are reduced to a pulp.

Next, they are mixed with a kind of glue, also procured from a plant.

Then the whole is again beaten till it becomes liquid, and can be poured into a vessel.

Moulds made of bamboo, and the shape of a sheet of paper, are plunged into the liquor.

The liquor sticks to the mould, because of the glue that has been put into it.

When it is dry, it becomes firm and glossy, and is, in fact, a sheet of paper.

The Chinese are so saving and thrifty, that they do not allow an atom of anything to be wasted.

When the paper has been written on, and, as we should think, done with, old people get their living by washing out the ink.

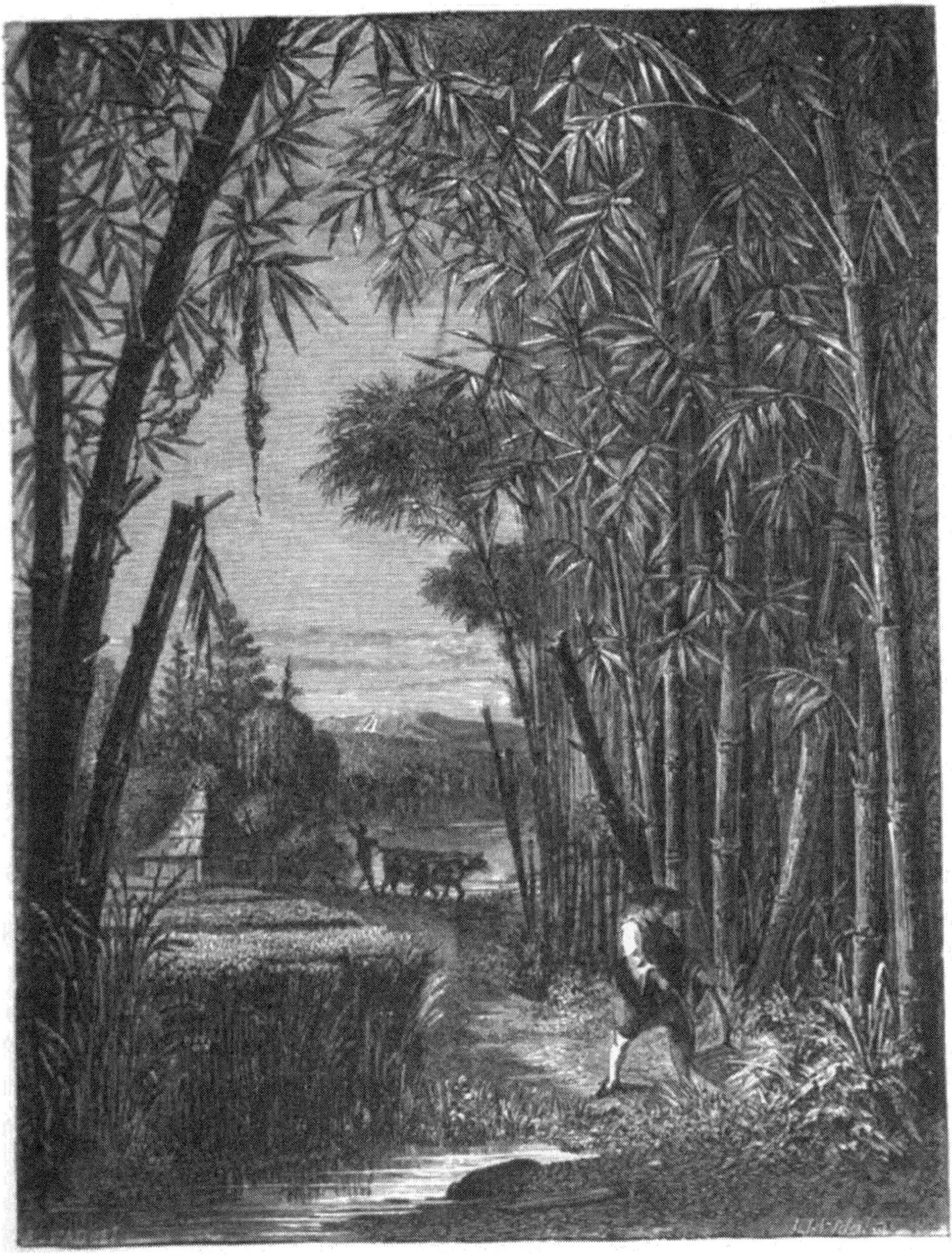

BAMBOO THICKET.

Then the paper is beaten and boiled, and made up into new sheets.

In the picture, you see the Chinaman busy in his plantation of bamboo.

I daresay that is his house, and that it is made of bamboo, and thatched with it, and all his furniture is made of bamboo as well.

THE CITY ON THE WATERS.

It is only within the last few years, that the English have been allowed to go into the city of Canton.

The Chinese do not like foreigners. They wanted to prevent them from coming into the country at all.

A beautiful river flows through Canton. It is as wide almost as a sea.

A great many people live on the river, and scarcely ever come on the land.

What do they live in?

Sometimes in wooden houses, which are built on stakes of wood, driven down into the mud at the bottom of the water. They look like the caravans we see going about at the fairs in England, only that they have posts instead of wheels. There are streets of these odd-looking houses with water between.

How do the people get about?

In boats. Numbers of people have no houses at all. They live all their lives long in boats.

The river is covered with boats. It is like a city on the waters.

There is every kind of boat you can think of.

The poor man cannot afford a very grand boat. His boat is only made of a few planks nailed to each other. He guides it about with a long oar called a scull, and he goes in and out among the other boats without getting upset.

The barber's boat is the smallest on the whole river. But he does a great deal of business. He has to keep in order the long tails of hair that hang down the backs of the Chinamen. And this gives him plenty to do

Every kind of food is sold on the river. There are boats full of live ducks and geese. They are let to go on shore and feed in the day-time, and fetched up at night. The people, who own them, live in a little wooden house in the middle of the boat. Almost every boat has a little wooden house in it.

The most beautiful boats are the flower-boats.

Here the house is rather grand, and has a carved door to it. Painted lanterns hang from the ceilings of the rooms. And there are pictures and looking-glasses, and all kinds of pretty things.

A rich Chinaman can have his boat, and make it as grand as he likes.

It is very noisy on the water among all the boats. Everybody cries his goods for sale, at the top of his voice. And music is played, and great gongs beat, and it is the strangest and busiest scene you can fancy.

A LITTLE ABOUT THE CHINAMAN'S RELIGION.

THE Chinese give a grand feast sometimes, but not to their friends. They give it to the gods.

Who are the gods?

They are idols of wood and stone. But the poor Chinaman prays to them, and does all he can to please them.

One night, an Englishman came into a city, and he saw a great light. One of the streets was lighted up in a most brilliant manner.

A table was set in the street, and the feast was going to be served. There were great dishes on the table, and sheep and pigs lay in them roasted whole. There were ducks and geese, and all manner of nice things.

Empty chairs were set round the table, and chopsticks laid, as if for company. And a band of music was playing to amuse the gods while they were eating.

When a little time had passed, the Chinese said the gods had done their feast.

Yet nothing on the table had been touched!

What became of the feast?

It was eaten up by the people.

People have not all the same religion in China.

Some people worship a man who lived two thousand years ago. His name was Confucicus.

CONFUCICUS.

While he lived, no one took much notice of him. But when he died, the Chinese began to build temples to him, and to pray to him.

Yet he was a poor sinful man like themselves.

Other people worship Buddha.

Who was Buddha?

Buddha was a man who pretended that he was changed into a god.

There are great images of Buddha in the temples.

There is another man still, whom the Chinese worship. He also lived a great many years ago. He said he could teach the people to walk through fire without being hurt, and keep them from dying.

But did he?

Oh no!

His words were none of them true. How could they be?

How glad we should be that missionaries can now go to China, and preach about Jesus Christ.

If the Chinaman would learn to read his Bible, he would soon cast his idols to the moles and to the bats.

THE TWO EMPERORS.

THE people of Japan live in three islands. But the three islands make only one empire.

Japan is not far from China, as you may see by looking at the map.

Europeans have only been allowed to go to Japan very lately. The Japanese do not like strangers, any more than the Chinese do. When an Englishman goes there, they run after him to look at him.

Japan is a beautiful country, because there are such lovely gardens to the houses. A Japanese can lay out a garden better than anybody.

He loves flowers, and has plenty of them in his house. And very splendid flowers grow in Japan.

Is there a king in Japan?

No; there is an emperor. But he is a curious sort of person. He lives shut up in a palace, with great gardens to it. No one ever sees him. He is too holy to be looked at!

Why is he too holy?

Because he pretends to talk to the spirits of people who are dead.

And if he likes, he can make a man a saint when he dies. When a man is made a saint, people pray to him as if he were a god.

Numbers of men are made saints in Japan. And there are a great many gods as well.

Who governs the people?

Another emperor, who is called the Tycoon.

This second emperor is almost as much shut up as the first. The people set spies on him, and will not let him go away from the city.

Once, some one gave him a present of a beautiful boat. But it was of no use. It would have been far beneath his dignity, to sail about in a boat.

He is very busy ruling his empire.

And sometimes he goes and pays the other emperor a visit.

An English lord went a little time ago to see the Tycoon, and make a treaty with him.

The English people wanted to trade with Japan.

The Tycoon could not speak English, so an interpreter had to repeat all that was said.

The interpreter was on his hands and knees on the floor. And every time he spoke, he touched the floor with his forehead.

He dare not stand up, in the presence of such a great man as the Tycoon.

THE BUTTERFLY TRICK.

In England men do not use fans. The climate is not hot enough to need them. But in Japan it is very hot indeed. The Japanese has two fans. One is called a war fan.

What! does he take it to battle with him?

Yes. If he has a few minutes' rest from fighting, he sits down and begins to fan himself.

The sheath of his fan is made of iron. If an enemy comes near, he can give him a hard blow with it. The sheath is as good as a weapon.

He does not use this great fan at home.

When he sits in his own garden, he fans himself with a very beautiful fan. It is so light, you could hardly feel it. But it makes a great deal of wind, as he moves it backwards and forwards.

Sometimes a man comes round to play tricks, and amuse the people in the streets and gardens.

One of his tricks is very pretty to look at. It is called the butterfly trick, and is done with a fan. First, he tears a piece of paper into two little bits. Each bit he twists into the shape of a butterfly. Then he puffs them into the air, and makes them look as if they were flying. They would come down again in a moment, for they are only paper. But he takes care not to let them.

He begins to fan gently, and the wind from the fan makes the butterflies flutter about as if they were alive. Sometimes, they seem to chase each other about. Then, they nearly touch each other. Next, they settle on the leaf of a tree, or on the fan itself. Then they fly away into the air, and go so far off, you think the wind from the fan can never reach them.

But it does. All their movements depend on the wind made by the fan.

It is a very curious and pretty sight. There were some Japanese in England, a little time ago, who went about to amuse and delight the people, by playing the butterfly trick.

FAMILY IN JAPAN.

In the picture, a family in Japan are having their breakfast. They are sitting on a mat. It would make them very uncomfortable indeed to sit on chairs.

SHOPPING IN JAPAN.

THERE are some grand shops in the streets of Yedo.

Yedo is the capital of Niphon.

And Niphon is the largest island in Japan.

At some of the shops silk dresses are sold, and all manner of splendid things.

The shop is open to the street, and looks like a great hall. There are counters for the shopmen to stand behind, and rows of shelves for the goods to lie upon.

The grand show-room is up-stairs.

JAPANESE LADY IN HER PALANQUIN

There are no chairs to sit upon. People sit on a couch covered with red cloth. The couch is called a divan.

Before any shopping can be done, the customer has to drink a cup of tea.

Drink tea!

Yes. The tea-shrub grows in Japan, as it does in China.

A servant will come up-stairs with a cup of tea and some pipes.

The customer sits quietly on the divan, and sips his tea, and takes whiffs at his pipe. All the time, he watches to see what the shopkeeper is doing.

The shopkeeper has not been idle.

The floor is soon covered with silks and satins of every colour. And there are crapes and gauzes, and every kind of dress you can wish for.

Where does the silk come from?

From Japan. The silk worm lives in Japan, as well as in China.

Some people like the silk made in Japan the best.

Are there any other shops?

Oh yes! a great many. There are shops where umbrellas are sold, for keeping off the sun. And there are fan shops, and shoe shops, where people buy shoes made of straw.

A Japanese always has his shoes made of straw. They soon wear out, and then he throws them away, and has a new pair. You may see old worn-out shoes, lying everywhere, by the side of the road.

Here is a Japanese lady riding in her palanquin.

She is allowed to go about the streets as she likes, and is not obliged even to wear a veil. But as soon as she is married, she will pull out her eyebrows, and blacken her teeth, and make herself look very ugly indeed.

What is that done for?

That no one may admire her except her husband.

It is one of the silliest customs in the world!

THE STEPPES.

ONCE, when Rome was a great city, and ruled over many countries, she had some very fierce enemies.

Tribes of savage people, who were fond of fighting, kept coming in great hordes to the very walls of Rome.

What were their names?

The Huns, the Mongols, and many other tribes.

If you read the history of Rome, you will hear of Atilla, the king of the Huns.

He was a very fierce man indeed. The little children in Rome used to tremble at the sound of his name.

Where did these people come from?

From a vast tract of country in the middle part of Asia.

Find the map and look for it. It is called Tartary.

The middle part of Asia is a great plain, high up above the level of the sea. It has in it mountains, deserts, and steppes.

You often hear of the steppes of Tartary.

What are they?

The steppes are plains that lie at the foot of hills. The word steppe is a Tartar word, and means a plain or prairie.

What people live there now?

The Tartars. There are many tribes of Tartars. The Mongol Tartar, the Calmuc Tartar, the Kirghis Tartar, and so on. But they all come from the fierce people who once fought with Rome.

The Mongol Tartars used to be a great nation. The Emperor of China had to build a wall to keep them off. It was one of the wonders of the world. It is said to have been fifteen hundred miles long. In places, it was so wide that six horsemen could ride abreast. Near the cities of China, the wall was built of solid stone. But in other parts, it was only built of mud and rubbish.

This great wall is standing now.

THE STEPPES.

Did it keep the Tartars off?

No. They contrived to conquer China in spite of the wall. The Emperor of China is a Tartar.

The Tartars had great cities once, but they are all gone. The ruins of one city are grown over with grass.

The Tartars are not any of them great, now. They are a wild race,

HORSEMEN IN THE STEPPES.

and very poor. They wander about, and live in tents, as the red men do.

The climate is very cold. The wind sweeps over the plains, and nearly freezes you to death. The east wind, that makes us shiver in the cold spring months, comes over Tartary. There are only two months of summer, in some parts of Tartary.

It is as bad as living in the frozen zone!

The rain will never come for a long time. Then the wind gets up, and blows the dust about so that you cannot see. In the middle of the day, it will be as black as night.

After the dust and wind, will come the rain. But it pours in such torrents that people quite dread it. The clouds seem to open, and the water rushes down with such force that all the fields and roads are under water. Hailstones will fall with the rain and kill a great many sheep.

The rain does almost as much mischief as the dry weather.

BRICK TEA.

SHOULD you like to hear a little more about the Tartars?

They are very much like the Chinese to look at. They have high cheek-bones, and very little eyes, and black hair. But they are not like the Chinese in their habits. They are very fierce, and love war and fighting, and like to roam about free as the air they breathe.

The Chinaman does not like fighting. And he is not at all fierce, and chooses to live in his own comfortable house. It would make him wretched to roam about as the Tartar does.

What does the Tartar live upon?

He has his flocks and herds. They feed on the grass that grows in the fertile places. When they have eaten it all up, the Tartar leads them somewhere else.

He is very fond of boiled mutton. The mutton is cooked in a very rough way. The sheep is cut into four quarters, and thrown into a great iron pot full of boiling water. It is boiled till it is done, and then the Tartars have their dinners.

They take the meat on their laps, and eat with their knives.

BRICK TEA. 187

VILLAGE IN THE STEPPES.

The water the mutton has been boiled in is called broth. The Tartars have bowls that they dip in, and they drink as much as they like.

The Tartar has plenty of milk, and plenty of tea.

The milk the Tartars like the best is not from the cow, but from the mare. And they will milk the sheep and the goats. The wife of a Tartar chief will go milking every day of her life.

Sometimes the women make the milk into a cake.

Shall I tell you how?

There are holes dug in the ground, and iron pots put in. A fire is made under the pot, and a boy stands by it, to keep it up with sticks and argols.

What are argols?

Little round balls of dried manure. The Tartar has often nothing else to make his fire of.

The milk is boiled in the pots, and stirred round as it boils. After a time it becomes thick like curd. Then it is cut into squares and dried in the sun.

People are glad to eat these cakes of dried milk or curd.

Then they have brick tea.

What can that be?

It is tea made into the shape of a brick.

It is not very good tea. The leaves were gathered last, after the best were gone. And they were not dried as the others were. They were wetted, and made to stick together with bullocks' blood. Then, they were pressed into a mould, and left to get hard. The tea is so hard and like a brick, that when a man wants some tea, he has to chop it off with an axe.

How does he make his tea?

He rubs it between two stones, and then throws it into the iron pot.

Is that all?

Oh no! He puts in a bowl of sour cream, a handful of meal, and a little salt. This is boiled for half an hour and served hot.

It is more like tea-soup than anything.

THE CAMEL OF THE TARTARS.

What animals live in Tartary?

A great many. I will begin with the largest.

There is the camel.

The Tartar camel has two humps.

Troops of camels wander about in the steppes. It is their home.

They are not at all fierce. If they see a man coming, they run to look at him. Then, when they have looked enough, they will go on eating.

They eat grass and shrubs, and all they can get.

The Tartar's riches are in his camel.

Sometimes he will eat the flesh of the young camel, and think it very nice. He gets plenty of milk from the mother camel, and it is as good as that of the cow. The skin of the camel is used for a great many purposes. It makes tents and clothing, and the harness for the horses. Leather, made from the skin of the camel, is as good as the leather we use in England.

THE CAMEL OF THE TARTARS.

The camel can go across the desert, and across those dreary places where nothing grows for it to eat.

The camel can go without eating or drinking for a very long time.

I will tell you the reason. The two humps on its back are really storehouses, where Nature has put a supply of food for it to live upon.

The hump is full of little cells, with a store of fat in each. When the camel has nothing to eat, the fat is drawn down into his stomach, and keeps him alive. But if he has to fast a long time, his hump will get thin, and lose almost all its fat.

When he does eat, he only wants a very little food. A handful of dried beans, or a few mouthfuls of what bushes or shrubs he can find as he goes along, will be enough for him.

So that it does not cost the Tartar much to keep a camel.

But how can the camel go without drinking?

It has a mass of cells or little pouches on the sides of its stomach. These are full of pure water. It can draw the water into its stomach, as it did the fat from its hump. So that it does not get thirsty.

Sometimes, a poor traveller, who is dying for want of water, has to kill his camel, and drink the supply in its pouches to save his life.

The camel can go a very long way without being tired.

It has just the kind of foot given it, that it will want.

Its foot is divided into two parts, or toes. The two toes are very long and strong, and have each a short nail.

The toes are joined together, near the ends, by a grisly membrane. Under the membrane is a thick and horny sole. The sole, in fact, of the camel's foot.

This large spreading foot, with its thick sole, can walk over the shifting sand of the desert.

Sometimes, even the strong patient camel may be made to walk too far. The sole of the foot wears out, and the flesh is laid bare. Then the Tartar puts shoes on his camel. The shoes are made of sheepskin, and do very well for a little time. But the poor camel is lame, and if it may not rest very soon, it lies down. Then nothing will induce it to get up again. The Tartar will have to leave it behind to die.

THE WILD HORSE OF THE STEPPES.

What other animals live in the Steppes?

The wild horse lives here, as it does in the prairies of North America. It is a rough-looking creature, with a shaggy coat, and its mouth and nose have long hairs growing from them, like the hairs of a goat.

THE WILD HORSE OF THE STEPPES.

It is of a brown colour, though sometimes you see a black or white horse.

The horses live in groups of twenty or thirty, and keep apart from their neighbours, each group feeding by itself. Unless an enemy comes in sight, when they all join together to drive him away.

THE WILD HORSE OF THE STEPPES.

Who are their enemies?

The wolves, or else the Tartars, when they come to catch fresh horses.

The wolves are very savage in the steppes. They come in a body and howl, and show their sharp white teeth. The strong full-grown horses put the little ones in the middle, and stand round them to protect them. They snort, and neigh, and kick with their hoofs, and are very angry. But it often happens that the wolves are too many for them. Then the poor horses take to flight, and many of them are killed by the wolves.

THE WILD HORSE OF THE STEPPES.

The Tartar hates the wolf, and will ride day after day to hunt him down.

He may well hate the wolf.

The wolf is more savage in Tartary than in any other country. Instead of running away from man, he will attack him. He will leave the cattle

TARTAR CATCHING A WOLF.

unhurt, and force his way into the house. Then he seizes the first person he meets by the throat.

When a wolf is seen prowling about, the Tartars mount their horses and ride after him.

They have long rods in their hands, with a cord at the end. The cord has a loop like a noose.

The man in the picture has flung it round the wolf's neck, and is dragging him off to be killed.

The Tartar is very kind to his horse, which he caught when it was running wild in the steppes. He rides about so much, that he may be said to live on horseback. He will eat and sleep without getting out of his saddle.

When he is not riding, he is sitting quite idle. He does not like work any more than the red man does. So, like him, the Tartar will always be poor.

It is the "hand of the diligent that maketh rich."

There are very few wells for the animals to drink from. Water is scarce in the steppes, and people have to go many miles in search of it. When a well is found, the Tartar shepherds water their flocks. A stone will sometimes lie on the well's mouth, and it has to be rolled back. The scene is just what it used to be in the days of the Patriarchs.

Do you remember Jacob watering the flocks of Laban?

The great herds of horses, and sheep, and goats, will be in a hurry to drink, and will push and jostle each other to get at the water. And sometimes, two of the horses will have a battle, and will gallop after each other over the plain.

And sometimes, a great camel will come marching up, and then the horses will be in a fright and run away; for the horse cannot bear to look at the camel.

The well will sometimes be very deep indeed. How do the shepherds get the water?

They draw it up in a bucket.

It is a curious sort of bucket. I do not think you ever saw one like it.

It is made of the entire skin of a goat. The skin was drawn off the animal whole, and the feet tied together, so that the water could not run through. The skin of the neck was the top of the bucket, and a rough kind of hoop was put in to hold it open.

The cord, that let down the bucket, was of twisted camels' hair.

There are no carpenters or rope-makers in the steppes.

"THE SON OF HEAVEN."

HAVE the Tartars a king?

No. But each tribe has a chief, who is called a king by his subjects. At the beginning of the year, these little kings take a very tedious journey into China.

What do they go for?

To prostrate themselves before the Son of Heaven.

This is the name by which the Emperor of China is called.

"THE SON OF HEAVEN."

The Emperor of China is far too grand a person to be looked at. On New-year's Day, he goes through the streets of Pekin to visit a temple where his ancestors are buried. But no one may peep out of the windows. The doors must be closed, and the people shut up in their houses, while he passes by. If a man were found in the streets, he would be put to death.

How different it is in England!

When the emperor gets to the temple, a herald calls out:—

"Let every man prostrate himself before the master of the earth!"

Now, the poor Tartar princes are all at the temple waiting for the emperor to come. As soon as the herald speaks, and before they have had time to catch a glimpse of his majesty, down they fall on the ground, and lie with their faces touching the earth. There are, perhaps, two hundred of them, and they lie in rows one behind the other. They dare not lift up their heads on any account. One prince who was in the front row, contrived to see a bit of the yellow robe of the emperor. But it was at the peril of his life! Meanwhile, the emperor passes between the rows of princes as they lie on the ground, and goes to bow before his ancestors. When he has done this, he comes out of the temple, passes the princes again, and goes back to his palace.

When he has fairly passed, the Tartar princes may get up again.

Was it worth while to come all the way from Tartary for this?

But the princes do get something for their pains. They think it a great honour to have prostrated themselves before the "Son of Heaven." And they have a sum of money given them. It is not much, and it is sometimes paid in bad money. But the poor princes dare not say a word about it. As for the emperor, he takes tribute from the Tartars, of camels and deer, and whatever their country can afford. And, in his heart, he looks upon them as his slaves.

THE PRAYING-MILL.

THE Tartars are not Christians, any more than the Chinese are.

They worship Buddha. Those who do not worship Buddha, worship the false prophet Mohammed. The priests of Buddha are called Lamas. They wear long yellow robes, with a red girdle and five gilt buttons. They have a collar of purple velvet, and a yellow cap with a red rosette. The Tartars are very fond of smart colours. A man, who is not a priest, and does not wear yellow, is called a black man. If he begins to speak about religion, people laugh at him. They do not allow any one to preach to them, except the Lamas.

What do the Lamas teach them?

They teach them to say a great many prayers. But the Tartar soon gets tired, and then he makes use of the praying-mill.

What is a praying-mill?

It is a machine the shape of a barrel. It turns round and round when it is pulled by a string. Sometimes it is placed where the wind can turn it without being pulled at all.

The mill is made of pasteboard, and has prayers stuck all over it. The prayers are written by the Lamas, and if they can be turned round and round, it is thought as good as praying.

A missionary once saw two men quarrel over a praying-mill. One of the men had come out and set it going. Then the other man came up and stopped it, and gave it a turn for himself. Upon this, the first man grew angry, and they were very near coming to blows.

But an old Lama settled the dispute, by turning the praying-mill for both of them.

What a mockery it is to call this prayer!

The Lamas live sometimes in great buildings called convents.

A man was riding near a convent on his mule with two camels behind him. The mule took fright and began to rear, and pulled at the camels so that they took fright as well. And all three set off at full gallop.

What was the matter?

A Lama, in his yellow robe, was lying all his length on the ground. His arms were stretched out, and his face touched the earth.

What was he doing?

He was going round the convent, and at every step he lay down in this way, all his length on the ground. You may think what a long time it would take him. He fancied he was doing a pious act, and that Buddha would be pleased with him.

THE TEMPLE OF GOLD.

It is very dangerous to travel about in Thibet. There are mighty mountains, and little ledges along the sides for people to walk on.

The mountains to the north of Thibet are called the Blue Mountains. Those to the south are called the Himalaya Mountains.

Thibet is hemmed in by mountains.
What people live in Thibet?
A tribe of Tartars live there.
Have the people of Thibet a king?
Yes; and a very curious person he is. He lives on the top of a rocky hill just out of Lassa.

Lassa is the chief town of Thibet. The palace is really a temple. There are several temples built together, and the king's temple is in the middle. It has a dome covered with plates of gold. And the pillars that support it are of gold. There is plenty of gold up in the mountains.

The Lamas from all parts of Tartary, and a great crowd of persons besides, come to the foot of the hill. They stretch themselves on the ground and worship. On high days and holidays, the king can look down and see them. There is a great avenue leading to the palace, and beautiful trees grow on either side. The avenue will be filled with pilgrims, come to worship as well. Some are on horseback, and some on foot.

They come to worship the king.
What! to worship a man?
Yes; they look upon him more as a god than a man. They say the spirit of Buddha dwells in him, and makes him holy.

The king has lived in that temple ever since he can remember. The Lamas brought him there when he was quite a baby.

Was he the son of the last king?
No; he was a child chosen by the Lamas.

There were three children brought for them to choose from. They cast lots to see which it was to be. The lots are put into an urn, and shaken. These lots are little gold fishes, with the name of a child on each.

The first name that is brought out is thought to be the right one. Then the poor little child is carried off to the temple of gold. He is brought up by the Lamas, and may never run about and play. He lives in the temple all his life, and has to sit on a cushion, and move his head, in a solemn manner, to the people who worship him.

The Lamas have houses close by, and do nothing but wait upon him.

Still, I think the great king of Thibet must often be very tired of his life.

Does Thibet belong to China?

No; it is a free country. Its great mountains protect it. The Chinese would like very much to conquer it, but they cannot.

A LITTLE MORE ABOUT THIBET.

THE people in Thibet do not roam about like the Tartars in the steppes. They live in houses, and have towns and villages.

Thibet is the richest, and yet the poorest country in the world.

It is rich in gold and silver. Shepherds pick it up in the crevices of the mountains. All the money used is silver. There are no copper coins.

But the people are very poor. Their houses are painted red and yellow, and made to look smart outside. But inside, they are wretched places. They are very dirty, and in such a litter you can hardly stir.

The people live on tea and black bread. They make their bread of barley. There is no wheat. The great mountains take up all the room, and leave very little for fields and pastures.

And as for the gold and silver, the Lamas get nearly all of it.

The climate is not pleasant. Those great mountains are tipped with snow. People, who go there in winter, are often frozen to death.

Once, a traveller was coming near a river, and he saw a herd of wild oxen in it. They looked as if they were swimming across. Their heads and great branching horns were above the water, but they did not move. When he came nearer he saw how it was. They had plunged into the water, just when it was beginning to freeze. It froze so fast and so hard, that the poor oxen were not able to stir. They were hemmed in with the ice and frozen to death.

The people of Thibet are obliged to have fires in their houses in winter to keep off the frost. The fire-place is nothing more than a basin of clay, in the middle of the room. A hole at the top of the ceiling lets out the smoke.

But nothing can get the roving Tartar of the steppes into a room. When he comes to an inn in Thibet, he likes to do just as he is used to do in his own wild country. He will set up his tent in the courtyard, and light his fire under it. In vain, the landlord tells him to cook his food at the stove in the kitchen. He will do nothing of the kind. Summer or winter, he likes to be in the open air. You could not make him more wretched than by shutting him up in a house.

THE YAK.

ALMOST every country, that I have told you about, has some animal given to it for its use and comfort.

In Thibet there is the yak.

The yak likes to live on the cold snowy mountains.

It has a clothing of soft curly hair almost like fur. Its tail sweeps the ground, and is of bright-coloured hair. It has horns like a cow, and there is a hump between the shoulders. Its legs are very short; and sometimes its long hair will trail on the ground, and give it rather an awkward look.

THE YAK.

It is not fierce, though it does not like to be meddled with.

The people of Thibet think the yak one of their greatest blessings.

The milk of the cow is very thick and rich, and there is a great quantity of it. It makes excellent butter.

The mother yak is so fond of her young one, that when it is taken from her, she will not give any milk.

The farmer's wife in Thibet knows what to do.

The young yak has been killed; but she brings its foot, and lays it down before the mother, for her to lick.

The yak seems quite contented; and as she goes on licking the foot, she gives her milk as usual.

The soft hair of the yak makes clothing. It is woven into a strong cloth.

The shepherds who pasture their flock, in these cold regions, wear a loose garment made of the hide of the yak. It hangs down to the knees, and is very warm and comfortable. At night they lie down upon it, and it serves them for a bed.

The long hair is made into a tent-cloth, and also into ropes. The long bright-coloured tail is used for an ornament.

Indeed, the whole wealth of some of the Tartar tribes in Thibet consists in the yak.

The yak goes up and down the mountains, and does not often stumble.

It carries burdens on its back; for the Tartars use it instead of a horse or a camel.

THE BUTTER FEAST.

WHAT kind of a feast can that be?

People in Thibet call it the feast of flowers. But it is not really so. It is a grand show of men and women, and animals, and flowers, and houses and gardens, all made of butter.

When the feast is going to take place, people come from all parts of Tartary and Thibet to see.

Caravans of pilgrims throng the roads leading to the town where it is held.

There is a convent of the Lamas at this town, and they have a great deal to do with it.

They are busy for three whole months before the feast begins. They have to make all the images, and grand things that are going to be shown.

From morning to night, they stand making up the butter into the shapes that are wanted. Every other minute, they dip their hands in water to keep them cool.

The feast is held in the depth of the winter, and you may think how their poor fingers ache with cold.

When the figures are made, they have to be painted. For they must appear in full dress.

The evening that the feast begins, the town is so full it can hardly hold the crowds who have flocked into it. Everywhere is heard the cry of the camel, or the lowing of the oxen. Outside the town, tents are set up for the pilgrims who cannot find room within.

Tartars of almost every tribe are come to the feast, and walk about in their native dresses. Some of them are busy going round the convent, and lying on the ground at every step, to please Buddha.

When all is ready, the sight is very curious indeed.

All the figures are placed on scaffoldings before the temples.

Red and yellow vases are put between them. It is dark, but no end of brilliant lights are set about to make the show dazzling.

The figures are some of them very large indeed. The animals look almost like life. There are tigers, and wolves, and sheep, and many others.

You could almost touch their fur to see if it was not real.

And there is Buddha himself, with a fair skin and long wavy hair.

And all these wonderful things have been made in butter!

All down the streets are little puppet-shows of butter. The puppets are dressed like Lamas, and all they do is to keep going backwards and forwards on the stage.

When the people have looked long enough at the figures and the shows, the fun of the evening begins. They dance and shout, and push each other about as if they were crazy. The Lamas go up and down with lighted torches, and try to keep the mob in order, and prevent them from knocking down the figures.

The feast does not last long. The next morning all is over. The butter figures are thrown away into a deep pit near the town. The trouble of three whole months is done away with in a single night.

Then the pilgrims set off home again, each to his own wild country. They walk in silence with their heads hung down.

A night of noise and riot is all they have had, for coming a long and tedious journey.

THE PEARL DIVERS.

THE beautiful pearls that you see worn in the hair, or round the neck, were once lying at the bottom of the sea.

The pearl was snugly hidden in the shell of an oyster, out of sight of everybody.

Near to the place, where the oyster lay, was an island called Ceylon. The people in the island knew that a great many oysters lay at the bottom of the sea. And each oyster was likely to have a pearl in its shell.

It is only one kind of oyster that has a pearl. The oysters we have in England are good to eat, but they have no pearls.

Once in the year, the people on the sea-shore are very busy indeed. You see they have a boat out, as if they were going to fish. And so they are; they are going to fish for oysters.

Do you see that man in the water?

He has a rope in each hand. The ropes are held fast by the people in the boat. They would not let go of the ropes on any account.

When the man has tight hold of the ropes, he puts his foot on a stone, which is tied to the rope. He has a bag with him to put the oysters in.

But how will he get the oysters?

He will pick them up from the bottom of the sea. He has been to the bottom of the sea many times, for he is a diver. Going down into the sea is called diving.

When all is ready, he holds his nose tight to prevent the water going in, and shuts his mouth.

THE PEARL DIVERS.

Then the people, in the boat, let him down into the sea.

Down, down, he goes, as quick as lightning! The water is rushing over his head, and in his ears. There are all kinds of strange things round him; but he has no time to look at them. He is at the bottom of the sea, and he begins to pick up oysters as fast as he can, and to put them into his bag.

THE PEARL DIVERS.

In two minutes he pulls the rope. He must get up again, or he will die. But the men hoist him up as quickly as they can. Up, up, he comes! He is quite breathless, but he soon gets better, and is ready to take another plunge.

There is a great fierce fish in the sea that goes swimming about, looking for what it can find to eat.

If it saw the poor diver it would snap his leg off. The diver is very much afraid of the shark.

In that country, people have not all learned to read the Bible. They do not know that God can take care of them in the sea, as well as on land. So they pay a man to keep off the sharks. This man is called a shark charmer, and he pretends that he can keep the sharks from coming near the divers. Of course he cannot; but the poor silly people believe him!

THE SPONGE AND THE CORAL.

Do men dive for anything but pearls?

Yes; they dive for the sponge, and they dive for the coral.

Where does the sponge live?

In the sea, on rocks, and sometimes in shallow pools of salt water.

It is an animal, though it does not look like one.

The great animal world that has in it lions and tigers and elephants, begins with the sponge.

The sponge has a soft jelly-like body, that drips away when it is brought out of the sea. You never see the body. The part of the sponge you see, is the framework or skeleton.

How do people get the sponge?

They have a fork with three prongs.

When the sponge is in shallow water, the man can stick the fork into it, and bring it out very easily.

But this kind of sponge is not very good, and it is sold much cheaper than the other.

The other sponge lives in the deep sea, and sticks to a rock.

A man must dive down to get it. And he cannot use his fork. The sponge is too delicate, and would be spoiled. He has to cut it from the rock with a knife.

What sea is the sponge found in?

In the Red Sea, on the north coast of Africa, and on the shores of Greece.

THE CORAL DIVERS.

The Greeks are very clever in diving for sponges.

Where is the coral found?

In the Mediterranean Sea, and in some places on the coast of France.

The coral divers come in a boat called the Coraline.

The diver has a great cross of wood, such as you see in the picture. To each arm of the cross, a net is hung like a sack.

The cross is lowered into the sea by itself, with the nets hanging to it. Then the diver goes down after it.

When he gets to the bottom, he begins to scrape the cross all along the rocks where the coral is to be found.

The coral branches get entangled in the nets, and in half a minute, diver, cross, and coral are all pulled up together.

THE MARK OF BUDDHA'S FOOT.

THERE is a story told about Buddha which the people of Ceylon believe.

They believe that when Buddha went away from Ceylon, he left the mark of his foot on the top of a high mountain.

The mountain is called Adam's Peak.

The people, who worship Buddha, think a great deal about the mark of his foot.

Once a year, they go up the mountain to look at it, and to give a present to Buddha.

It is no easy matter to climb up to Adam's Peak. The mountain is very steep, and the cone at the top rises like a sugar-loaf. The people have to get to the top of the cone before they can see the mark of Buddha's foot.

There is a little stream at the bottom of the cone, and here the pilgrims stop and bathe. Then each pilgrim takes the handkerchief from his head and wraps his present in it. He carries his present on his head. The present consists of a few coins of money, or a little rice, or cocoa-nuts, or even flowers.

When the stream has been passed, the road gets very steep indeed.

In the steepest places, steps are cut in the rock, to help the pilgrims along.

At length, very tired and panting, the pilgrims reach the top of the cone.

THE MARK OF BUDDHA'S FOOT.

What do they see?

A very splendid view half over the island.

But this is not what they look at.

What they look at, is a little wooden shed fastened to the rock, and with a wall built round it.

If it were not for the great iron chains that hold the shed to the rock and to the wall, it would be blown away by the wind.

The shed is decked out with flowers, and is thought to be a very holy place. Under it, is the mark said to have been made by the foot of Buddha.

It is a very large mark, but not much like a foot. It has a gilt border round about it. People say that Buddha planted one foot on Adam's Peak, and with the other stepped over to India.

The pilgrims do not go into the shed. They stand and look at the mark, and keep bowing themselves, and putting the palms of their hands together, and raising them over their heads.

All the while, they keep muttering prayers. Then they lay their presents down, and the priest puts them, for a few minutes, on the mark of the foot.

After this, the pilgrims go a little lower down the mountain, and one of them reads aloud from a book.

The book tells them not to steal or kill, or to tell a lie. But it is not like the Bible.

The Bible tells us that God's Holy Spirit can give us new hearts, so that we may not wish to steal, or kill, or tell a lie.

There is nothing like this in Buddha's book.

What becomes of the presents?

The chief priest gets them. He lives at Candy, the chief town of Ceylon, and the presents are sent to him.

The priests in the shed do not live on the mountain. The peak is often covered with thick clouds, and no one could get up to it.

It is fine weather when the pilgrims come, and then the priest is able to stay in his shed.

It is more dangerous to come down the peak, than to get up. The path has no steps on this side the mountain. But chains are put, like a balustrade, for the pilgrims to take hold of.

If you gave a look down, the view is very dreadful. The road seems as if it hung in the air.

THE ELEPHANT.

So many elephants are brought to England, to be carried about in wild beast shows, that I daresay you have seen one.

It has a dark-coloured skin, all over wrinkles and folds, long flapping ears, and a trunk that it uses as a hand.

It could pick up a pin from the floor with its trunk.

The elephant loves the deep shady forests of Ceylon. It chooses out a place where there is water, for it cannot live without its bath. It will stand for hours, in the water, under the great trees, flapping its ears; or else it will fill its trunk with water and squirt it over its body.

When it is hungry there is plenty of nice food close at hand. It eats the tender young shoots of the trees or the leafy boughs. It pulls them down with its trunk.. I am afraid it pulls down and destroys a great deal more than it eats.

On fine moonlight nights, the elephant often fancies he should like a little change. He will go trampling on, with his great feet, into the fields of rice and corn. There will be a fence round the field, but it is not of much use. He will break it down, and soon get in. Perhaps some other elephants will have come with him, for he likes company, and they will have a fine feast on the corn, or whatever they can find.

Before it is light the next morning, they will have gone back to the forest.

But the marks of their great feet, and the mischief they have done, will be left behind.

The people of Ceylon often hunt the elephant. They are angry with

THE ELEPHANT.

him for spoiling their nice fields and gardens. And they want to get those long shining tusks of his, that are made of ivory.

Or else, they want to set him to work, and make him fetch and carry, and be a kind of slave to them.

An elephant can do all kinds of work, and is very quick at being taught.

How do they catch the elephant?

Sometimes they go into the forest, and shoot him with guns. But if they want to catch a great many elephants together, they make a corral.

What is a corral?

A great place fenced round with strong stakes, so strong that even the elephant cannot break them. The corral has an opening for the elephants to get in, and another opening where they fancy they can get out. But they are mistaken. This second opening leads them to a narrow place, where they cannot turn round, and in which they are caught.

For the people who are hunting, fasten up the opening directly the elephants have gone in.

The elephants would not go into the corral at all, if they were not driven by fright. The hunters light fires all round the place where the elephants are feeding. And they make

ELEPHANTS CAUGHT IN THE CORRAL.

loud cries, and beat drums, so that the elephants begin to run. There is but one way left open for them to run, and that leads to the corral.

THE TIGER HUNT.

CEYLON is a very beautiful island. The air is sweet with flowers and spices. There are woods, and groves, and rivers. And there are blue mountains, in the distance, where people can go, when it is very hot weather, and be quite cool and comfortable.

The more white people go to live in Ceylon, the fewer wild beasts there will be. White men have plenty of courage, and they will try to get rid of the wild beasts, and then it will be as safe to walk about in Ceylon, as it is in England.

Are there many wild beasts in Ceylon?

Yes. But there is one which is the most savage and cruel of them all. I mean the tiger.

There is a part of the forest called jungle. Shrubs and tall rank grass grow, and make a kind of wilderness. It is there the tiger lurks.

He will crouch so near to the ground, that his body cannot be seen; and he will creep about in the jungle without making any noise! But woe be to the poor animal who passes that way! It will not know the tiger is there, until he springs out upon it!

The people in Ceylon dread the tiger more than anything. If they know a tiger is lurking about the village, they will try to hunt him down, before he has done a great deal of mischief.

Sometimes, they go to hunt him on the back of an elephant.

There is a little car put on the back of the elephant. It is called a howdah. And the men, well armed with guns and spears, get into it.

They have had to give the elephant a few lessons beforehand. They have made him look at a stuffed tiger, and let him trample it under his feet. But the elephant has such a dread of the tiger, that, in spite of all his teaching, he may run away at the sight of him.

THE TIGER HUNT.

When the hunters get to the forest, it often happens that the tiger will be lurking, as usual, in the jungle. He is a great coward, and will perhaps slink away if he thinks he shall get the worst of it. But if he is very hungry, or if a shot from the gun wounds him, he will spring out in a rage and give a great roar.

The roar frightens the elephant, and he often tries to run away. But his driver will make him turn round, and face the tiger.

The elephant is afraid that the tiger will hurt his trunk, and he holds it up in the air. Sometimes, he will give the tiger a great blow with his trunk, so that he is half killed. But often the tiger, who is very nimble, and springs like a cat, will jump on the side of the elephant, and hang by his claws. This is a moment of great danger, for in another instant he will be in the howdah. But the men have had their guns ready this long time, and they fire them off. Then the tiger will drop down dead. But the elephant has had such a fright, that he dare not carry the tiger on his back, even when he has been shot.

HUNTING THE TIGER.

THE TALIPOT.

THERE is a very noble tree which grows in Ceylon.

It is a palm, and is called the talipot. The talipot has a straight stem, and grows to the height of two hundred feet.

Only think what a tall tree it must be!

Its beautiful green leaves are like a fan. They can be opened and shut just as you please. When the leaf is open, it is so large that thirty men can stand under it.

But it is not at all heavy to carry. Even when it is wide open it can be lifted about with ease. You may think what a capital umbrella the leaf of the talipot makes. The soldiers, who are marching along the country, use it to keep off the sun and the rain.

The rain cannot get through the leaf, if it comes ever so fast. The soldier's umbrella is waterproof.

There is another capital thing about the leaf of the talipot.

It is so large that it makes a tent. Many a traveller in Ceylon, has found shelter by setting up the leaf of the talipot, and getting under it.

Once, in the old days of Ceylon, if a man had a number of talipot leaves carried before him, he was known to be a grandee.

They used to be carried shut up like a fan.

Does the talipot bear any fruit?

Yes; but not till the last year of its life.

Then, a cluster of lovely yellow blossoms comes out at the top, and spreads in great branches.

The bud of the flower has a hard rind or sheath. When the flower is ready to come out, the rind bursts with a great noise.

Then the flowers come out; but they smell so strong that the people who live too near cannot bear it. So they cut down the tree, before the flowers have time to come out.

The fruit is not good to eat. But the stem is full of a pith like meal, that can be made into very nice bread.

THE HUMMING-BIRD.

UNDER the shade of a tree, at the end of one of the twigs, hangs a tiny little nest. It hangs in the air, and is as light as a feather. It is made of moss, and down, and whatever the bird could find. It is very snug, and two tiny eggs the size of peas, and as white as snow, lie within it.

Watch a moment, and we will see what bird it is, that has built the nest. She has only gone to have a sip of honey. It is a lovely place to watch in. Flowers scent the air. Yonder is a deep wood. Scarlet cactuses grow all about, and strange flowers of all shapes and sizes. Some are like monkeys, some like bees, some like butterflies. These flowers are called orchids. The orchids grow in England, only not nearly so large. This place is many miles from England.

Hark! the bird is coming. It is the tiniest bird you ever saw. Its body is no bigger than a nut. But its feathers are more lovely than I can describe. It has a green crest, on its head, which sparkles like a little star. The colours on its body are green, and gold, and purple. You can scarcely tell where one ends, and another begins.

If you look about, you will see plenty more of these little creatures. They are called humming-birds. They live in many places where it is hot. They live in India, and in

HUMMING-BIRDS SIPPING HONEY.

14 a

America. The woods and groves are alive with them. They flash about here, and there, clad in all the colours of the rainbow. The eye is never tired of watching them.

The humming-birds, in the picture, are hatching their eggs. When the

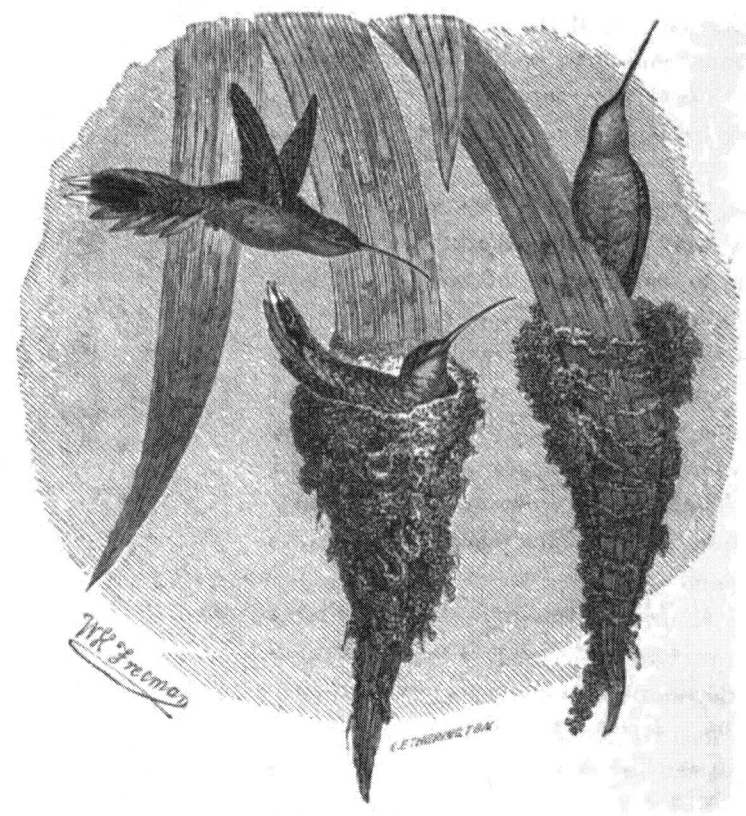

HUMMING-BIRD ON HER NEST.

mother bird is tired, her mate comes and takes her place. Then she springs up, and darts away into the woods.

She chooses some flower that has honey in it. She hovers in the air, and moves her wings about so quickly, that you can hardly see them. Her wings make a humming sound as she hovers over the flower.

Does she want the honey?

Yes; she will finish her dinner with a sip of honey. But she is thinking now about the insects.

There are a great many insects hidden at the bottom of the flower. She spies them out, with that bright eye of hers. Then she darts her long tongue into the middle of them. An insect sticks to it, for the tongue is sticky, as if it had been rubbed with glue. The insect is drawn into her mouth. She swallows it, and then darts out her tongue for another. All this time, she is hovering over the flower, and humming with her wings. When she has had enough insects, she sips a little honey, and flies back to her nest.

THE SNAKE-CHARMER.

A MAN came one day to a village in India.

Should you like to know how he was dressed?

He did not want much clothing in that hot country.

He wore a turban on his head, and a piece of white cloth loosely wrapped round his body. That was all.

The man had a brown skin, like the rest of the people in India. He was going about to get his living. He was called a Hindoo.

His trade was to be a juggler, or a snake-charmer. He could do both. He had a basket, in his hand, with some snakes inside it. He stopped at a house, and asked if the people had any snakes.

In India, snakes creep into the houses and hide themselves in some hole or corner. Many of the snakes have poison in their fangs. If they bite a man, he dies very quickly. The master of the house, perhaps, tells the juggler that he has no snakes. But what does the cunning juggler do?

He contrives to take a snake, out of his basket, and pop it into a hole without any one seeing. Then he puts a rude kind of pipe or flute to his mouth, and begins to play upon it. The snake, that has been popped into the hole, hears the music. It rears up its head, and wriggles itself out upon the floor. The juggler snatches it up, and puts it into his basket.

THE SNAKE-CHARMER.

THE SNAKE-CHARMER.

Of course, the master of the house does not know that the cunning juggler has ever seen the snake before.

He thinks it very wonderful that the snake should not bite.

But the snake is quite tame, and very likely has had its poison fangs taken out.

If a fresh snake comes out, which it sometimes does, enticed by the music, the juggler does not mind. He knows how to take hold of it so that it cannot hurt him. And he can soon beat out the fangs that have the poison. Then, it is popped into the basket and made tame.

When the juggler has finished his work, and been paid for it, he takes up his basket and goes on to the next village. Is he going to catch more snakes? No; he is going to make the snakes dance.

He chooses an open space in the village, just before the houses. Then he sets down his basket, and begins to play on his flute.

When he has played a minute or two, the lid of the basket is pushed up. A snake rears its head, and begins to look about it. Its bright eyes sparkle and shine, as if the sound of the music pleased it. And it moves its body backwards and forwards, to the tune the juggler is playing.

The people in the village get round him to look. They think it a very wonderful thing to see the snake dance.

Is that all he does?

Oh no! He will take hold of a snake with his bare hand. He will even twist it round his neck, as you see him doing in the picture.

Then he puts its mouth to his cheek, and plays all sorts of tricks with it. The people are very much delighted, though I daresay they have seen the performance many times before.

THE TURTLE.

THE turtle's great body is so soft and helpless that it would be sadly off without its shield. Nature has given it a thick heavy shell, that covers it all over. It can draw its head and feet under the shell, and be quite safe.

It has a great many enemies. When it was a very little turtle, and had just come out of the egg, it ran down to the sea. The turtle lives in the sea, though it was not born there. Its mother laid her eggs in the sand, scooping out a place for them. And the warmth of the sun hatched them. So the turtle first saw the daylight on shore.

It was a weak little creature in those days. And the rough waves drove it back, and gave it a rude buffet. And the sea-birds hovered overhead, ready to pounce down upon it. And the wild beasts came to look after the young brood of turtles, and to devour as many as they could. So you see the poor little turtle had something to do, to escape from all its enemies.

CATCHING THE TURTLE.

But its greatest enemy was man. As it grew larger and stronger, it became fit for food. Its flesh was tender and delicate. The sailors out at sea, who had to eat salt beef every day, liked to touch at the place where turtles could be found. Rich people in England liked to feast on turtle

THE TURTLE.

soup. So that ships had to bring home as many turtles as the men could catch. And they were sure to get well paid for their trouble.

How do people catch the turtles?

In several ways.

They watch for the mother turtle to come on shore, and lay her eggs. She does this in the night, and as secretly as she can.

The men hide themselves, and listen till they hear the turtles coming. Then they keep quiet, for if the turtle heard the least noise, she would hurry back to the sea.

She stands still and listens. If no sound is heard, she begins to scoop with her fore-feet, and dig a hole in the sand.

While she is busy the men rush upon her, and turn her on her back. It is hard work to do this, and takes a great many men. But once on her back, she cannot get up again, and they leave her, and go to turn over as many more turtles as they can.

There is another way of catching the turtle. Men go out in a boat, as you see in the picture, and look for the turtle. Sometimes, it is seen to rise to the surface of the water for air. Then a man, who can swim well, jumps into the sea, and fastens a rope round the neck or the foot of the turtle. He is very quick and dexterous, and the turtle is heavy and slow. Then he swims back to the boat, and the men pull all together, and soon get the turtle on board.

The boat in the picture is called a proa. The head and the stern are both alike.

The proas are used by the people of the Ladrone Islands, and are so swift that they can go twenty miles an hour.

THE BANIAN TREE.

ONE day, a bird flew over the forest. As it flew, it dropped a seed into the crown of beautiful leaves that grow at the top of the palm-tree. The bird flew away, and the little seed lay there as if forgotten. Under the hot sun and warm rains, the little seed began to sprout.

It put forth first one rootlet and then another, until at last, it was fixed firmly in the crown of dark handsome leaves.

The palm-tree was its home, the only place it had to grow in. Presently, the roots became larger, and began to descend. They wound themselves round and round the palm-tree like a net.

The palm-tree grew in the forest, and reared its stately head among the trees. For a time, it was stately as ever. But the roots that had taken hold upon it, began to clasp it tightly. The sap could not move about as it used to do. The palm-tree drooped, and hung its head. Still, the roots kept their hold. They had reached the ground, and were as firmly fixed in the earth as the palm-tree had been. In fact, the palm-tree was dying, while the roots were living and thriving. The roots belonged to a kind of fig-tree, called the banian.

The banian is a very curious tree indeed. It does not often grow by being set in the ground, as other trees do. It has two ways of being set and of growing.

One is, by the birds of the air dropping the seed, as I have just told you. The other way is more curious still.

When the tree is fully grown, it begins to send down long slender shoots. At first they sway about in the wind. But by-and-by, they grow long enough to touch the ground. Each slender shoot will strike its rootlets in the soil, and become a stem. You can see these stems in the picture. Some are thick and strong, and become like so many props to the old tree. Others have not yet reached the ground, but are swaying loosely about.

Year by year, the banian, with its props, keeps on growing. At length it gets very large indeed. Its branches spread out far and wide. It will have as many as a hundred props. And seven thousand men can rest beneath its shadow!

What a very great tree it is, to be sure!

THE BANIAN TREE.

In that hot country, how gladly do men and animals welcome the broad-spreading shade!

The poor tired Hindoo sits under it to rest. He is so anxious for the props to grow, that he ties wet moss on the branches. The moisture makes a shoot begin to bud. Then, he makes a little case of bamboo for it to go in, and waxes it down to the ground. It very soon takes root. At first it is only like a slender cord. But it gets thicker and thicker, and becomes a stem.

Sometimes, the herdsman makes his hut of the banian-tree. Under the burning sky of India, he is glad to find such a cool retreat. He sets to work to weave the branches together, and fill up the space between the stems.

Very soon he has made himself a shady dwelling, where he can sit and look out upon his flock.

THE GREAT SPIDER.

The little humming-bird, that glitters in the sun, has a very frightful enemy. This enemy will set a trap for him, and the poor little bird will flutter in. Once in, there is no chance of getting out again.

The trap is a strong thick web, woven by a spider.

Can a spider catch a bird?

Yes; there is a kind of spider that can. Indeed, it is called "the bird-catching spider."

It makes a little tunnel for itself to live in, and lines it with a white substance like muslin. Here it lies in wait for its prey, and is ready to pounce out upon any poor little bird that gets entangled in its net.

The spider is quite a monster to look at. Its legs are as thick as a quill; and it is covered all over with coarse hairs. If you touched the hairs they would run into your fingers, and make them smart and tingle for several days.

There is one kind of bird-catching spider, that is not content to wait at home for its prey. It goes out hunting. It will climb the trees, and hide itself under the leaves.

If it can find the nest of the humming-bird, it will soon devour the little ones. And if it sees the mother bird coming, it will dart upon her, and seize her with its great claws.

The poor little humming-bird can never get away, if she is once caught.

Where do these great spiders live?

In India, and South America.

A traveller, in South America, wanted to bring one of these spiders home with him.

He asked some Indian children to catch one for him.

The next day, he saw them bringing the spider to him.

How do you think they brought it? They had tied a string round its body, and were leading it along as if it had been a dog.

THE FLY-CATCHERS.

THERE is a tribe of little birds that are often hunted by the great spider. He is always on the look-out for them. He can catch them as easily as he does the humming-birds.

They are called fly-catchers.

If you look at the frontispiece, you will see some of them. They have hung their nest to the end of a twig. It is a tiny cup, made of down. The bird picked up the down as it floated in the air.

Where did the down come from?

From a tree called the silk-cotton tree.

There are seed-pods all over the tree. When they burst, the silky down comes out, and is carried about by the wind.

It is not used as cotton, for it is not strong enough. But hundreds of little birds dart after it, and carry it away in their bills to make their nests.

The fly-catcher is as beautiful as the humming-bird. Her body is so tiny that it is no bigger than the tip of your finger. It is as light almost as a feather.

She can sport amongst the water-lilies without making a ripple. When she settles on the leaves of the sensitive plant, they do not shrink. Her weight can hardly be felt.

A large, bright flower, such as you meet with in the tropics, would make the little fly-catchers a tent.

But neither the fly-catchers nor the humming-birds are all the same size. I have been telling you of the smallest kind.

There is one species which is quite a giant among them. It is nearly as large as a sparrow.

The wings of the fly-catcher are of the most brilliant colours. Sometimes they are of a vivid green, and then she is called an emerald; or she will be compared to a ruby, or a diamond, or any other precious gem.

She lives in the burning heat of the tropics, and her food is insects.

Thousands upon thousands of fly-catchers glisten and shine in parts of the forest where man could not live. He dare not brave the dangers he would meet with in these recesses. The air is unhealthy and full of poison. He would die of fever in a short space of time. There are venomous snakes, and poisonous plants, and savage beasts. But, in spite of all the dangers, the bright fly-catchers revel, and are in their glory.

Among the decaying stems, and growing sometimes upon them, are the gayest and most fantastic flowers. The fly-catcher hovers over them. Her wings move so quickly you cannot see them. Her body all the time is still and motionless. Then her long bill is plunged into the depth of the flower, and an insect drawn out, or a sip of honey taken.

The bird is a passionate little creature. If the flower has been emptied of its sweets, she goes into a rage. She will tear the bright petals to pieces, and scatter them to the winds.

One of the fly-catchers is very fond of bees, as well as of honey.

He lives in America, and is called the tyrant fly-catcher.

He will take his stand on some twig or fence, near a row of bee-hives, and watch for the bees to come in and out. Then, he will pounce down upon them, one after the other, and eat them up.

The owner of the bee-hive gets very angry at having all his bees eaten. He fetches his gun, and lies in wait for the fly-catcher, and if he can, he shoots him.

In spite of the fly-catcher's love for bees, he is really very useful.

When his mate is sitting on her eggs, he will drive away any enemy that comes to molest her.

THE FLY-CATCHERS.

If his nest is near the farm-yard, no eagle, or hawk, dare come and carry off the farmer's chickens. Out will dart the brave little fly-catcher and attack him fiercely. Sometimes he will mount on the eagle's back and peck him with great violence, and torment him so much, that he will be only too glad to get away.

A VIPER PURSUED BY THE BIRDS.

There is a deadly snake in the tropics, called the lance-headed viper. It makes no noise to give people warning. It glides along under the leaves and bushes, and can neither be seen nor heard. People dread it more than any other snake, because they come upon it unawares. But an army of bright little birds are their greatest friends.

No sooner does a fly-catcher or a humming-bird spy out a lance-headed viper than it sets up a shrill cry.

The birds know what it means, and they fly out in a body. Nightingales, thrushes, humming-birds, and all the little fly-catchers, make quite a crowd. They hunt the viper, and drive him before them. In vain he darts out his forked tongue : they are above him, out of his reach. They let him have no rest. In vain he tries to hide himself : they follow him with their shrill cries.

It is as if they were calling to man, and saying, "Come, come! we have found him! our enemy and yours!"

THE NUTMEG AND THE CLOVE.

THERE are some beautiful islands in the East Indies. They are called the Spice Islands.

A great many spices grow there.

The clove comes from the Spice Islands. The clove-tree is very handsome to look at. It is a little like the bay-tree, and its leaves are like the laurel. The flowers grow in bunches quite at the end of the branches, and are of a delicate peach-like colour. When the flower begins to fade, the calyx or outer cup turns yellow, and then red. It is shaken from the tree, and falls with a seed inside it. The seed is oval, dark-coloured, and of a large size. This seed is the clove, and has to be dried in the sun.

When the cloves come to England, we think them very nice in our apple-puddings and pies.

The clove-tree smells of cloves in the most delicious manner. The air is quite loaded with its spicy fragrance. But it is a long time before it has any fruit upon it. The owner of a plantation has to wait, sometimes as long as nine years, before he gets any cloves. Another spice that we use very much in our cookery is the nutmeg. The nutmeg grows, now, in more places than one. But it used to grow only in the Spice Islands.

These islands belonged to the Dutch, and they wanted to keep all the nutmeg-trees to themselves, and prevent them growing anywhere else.

Indeed they rooted a great many of them up. They were afraid the trees might spread and become too common, and that people in other countries might begin to trade in nutmegs.

But the Dutch could not carry out their selfish scheme. A bird of the air prevented them, and carried the nutmeg to a great many places quite out of their reach.

This bird was the spice-eating pigeon. It used to feed on the nutmeg, and swallow it whole.

The nutmeg passed through its body, and dropped, sometimes in one place, and sometimes in another.

Where it dropped it began to grow. Many of these places did not belong to the Dutch, so the nutmeg began to spread in spite of them.

The pigeons that live in the Spice Islands, and feed upon the nutmegs, get so fat, that when they fall to the ground they burst.

The nutmeg is the kernel of the fruit; the mace is the husk or outer covering. So that we get mace and nutmeg from the same tree.

The mace is of a beautiful red colour. The redder it is, the better it is thought to be.

It is dried, and then packed in bags and sent to Europe.

The nutmeg-tree is still more beautiful than that of the clove. Its leaves are green outside and gray beneath. But, like the clove, it is a long time before it begins to bear any fruit.

THE BIRD OF PARADISE.

A VERY beautiful bird lives in the fragrant woods of the Spice Islands. It is called the bird of Paradise. The people, who live in that country, think there is no bird half so beautiful to be found anywhere.

And if you had ever seen one, you would think so too.

The feathers of its head and neck are as soft as velvet, and of a golden colour, that changes with every changing light.

THE BIRD OF PARADISE.

You see what a splendid plume of feathers it has for a tail. They are white and yellow, and as light and fairy-like as possible.

The birds of Paradise fly a great many together in a flock. One bird goes first, and is in fact the leader. The natives call him the king.

BIRD OF PARADISE.

He seems to show the other birds the way, for they fly after him, and settle where he settles.

They take care to fly against the wind. Their long feathers are then blown behind them, and do not come in their way. And they like to fly very high; for if a storm of wind comes on, the air is calmer the higher they mount up.

The leader, or king, is rather different from the rest of the flock.

He has some spots upon the feathers of his tail.

The people who live in the Spice Islands know him by his spots. They often go into the woods to shoot the birds of Paradise, and they try to shoot the leader first.

They make a little bower of leaves and boughs to hide themselves in. Then they get inside it, and watch. The poor birds do not know that any one is there, and they come perching about upon the branches.

Then out flies an arrow, and strikes one of them dead. And then comes another arrow, and another, till the hunter thinks he has birds enough, and need not kill any more.

He takes home the poor dead birds, and gets them ready for sale. He stuffs them with spices, and cuts off their legs. Then he can sell them to Europeans.

Once a silly tale got abroad, that the bird of Paradise had no legs, and that it never settled on the ground, or ate anything but dew.

Indeed, this was why its name was given to it.

The reason of this silly story was, that all the birds of Paradise had their legs cut off.

INSECTS THAT GIVE LIGHT.

You have often heard of the glow-worm in England. She gives out a bright little spark of light, like a star on the ground.

She does it to let her mate know where she is. Her mate has wings, and is flying about in the air. The glow-worm gives a very feeble light compared to some other insects.

There is a curious lantern sometimes used in these countries, which gives so much light that people can work by it, as we should by a lamp.

What gives the light?

Not oil, not gas, not a candle. No! The light comes from insects. A number of beetles are shut up in the lantern. They shine and sparkle, and give all the light that is wanted.

People, in these countries, are very glad of these shining insects. They make use of them in a great many ways.

INSECTS THAT GIVE LIGHT.

If a man is going along in a dark night, he will fasten a beetle to each foot, in order to see the road.

The black women are very fond of being smart. They put the shining insects in their hair. When it is dark, the insects sparkle like so many jewels.

When a girl is going to a dance, she will sometimes stick the beetles all over her dress.

As she dances and glides about, she will look as if her dress was made of fire.

There is a great fly called a lantern-fly, that gives a bright light from its head.

Its head is large and long, and marked with red and green. When night comes, its great head will be in a blaze of light. You could see to read the smallest print by it.

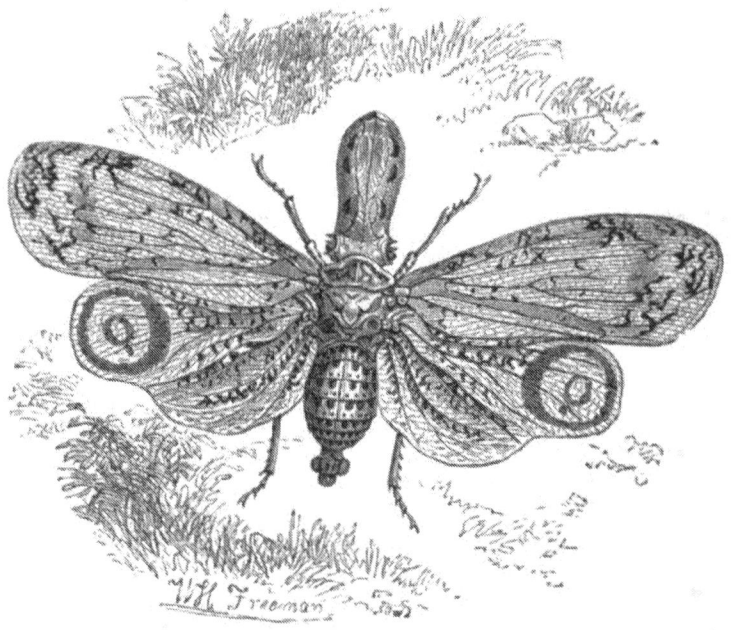

LANTERN FLY.

If a man wants a torch, he has only to tie a few lantern-flies to the top of a stick, and he has as good a torch as he could wish for.

A lady once had a present made to her, of a box of lantern-flies.

In the night, these flies made such a noise that she got out of bed, and lighted a candle to see what was the matter.

But when she opened the box, she dropped her candle in a fright. The inside of the box seemed all in a blaze. Each fly looked as if its head were on fire.

Of course the insects got out of the box, and began to fly about the room.

Then she saw where the light came from, and she soon set to work to catch them again.

Where do these shining insects live?

In the tropics; in India and America.

THE HINDOO GOLDSMITH.

I AM going to tell you about another Hindoo, who goes from house to house to get his living.

He has a better trade than that of the juggler.

He is a goldsmith, and can make necklaces and bracelets, and all manner of trinkets. He comes to a house, and brings his tools with him. He will work all day for half a rupee, which is about a shilling of our money.

What are his tools?

A little forge, in which he means to light a fire of charcoal. A little pan, the shape of a saucer, to hang over the fire, and to melt his gold in. He calls it a crucible. He has a pair of pincers to take hold of the gold; a hammer, and an anvil. His anvil is merely a piece of flint in an iron frame. He will beat out the gold upon it, as the blacksmith beats the iron.

The owner of the house gives him the gold, and tells him what trinkets he wishes it to be made into. People in India are very fond of trinkets, though they are not always made of gold or silver.

A great many of them are sham trinkets, and are made of brass and pewter. But such as they are, the natives wear as many as they can. They have rings round their ankles as well as on their fingers.

THE HINDOO GOLDSMITH.

The women in the picture have their anklets on. And a Hindoo woman will wear a ring in her nose. So that the goldsmith finds plenty to do.

When all is ready, he sets to work and lights his fire. Then he puts the gold into his crucible, and begins to melt it. He has a hollow pipe or tube that he uses instead of a pair of bellows. He thrusts one end of the tube under the crucible, and blows with all his might into the other. This makes the fire blaze up very quickly, and the gold soon begins to melt.

HINDOO WOMEN WITH ANKLETS ON.

While the gold is melting, he plays a cunning trick in order to get some of it. I am afraid he is not any more honest than the juggler. He throws a kind of acid into the crucible. This makes the gold give a great fizz, and boil over into the fire. Some of it runs among the charcoal, and lies there snugly hidden. When the goldsmith gets home he can pick it out at his leisure. People know very well that the goldsmith will cheat them if he can. But he is so quick and cunning, that they never catch him in the act.

When the gold has been melted and beaten, he begins to make it up. His fingers are small and nimble, and they can do almost anything. He makes such beautiful chains, and rings, that the people of the house are delighted. And if they suspect he has made away with some of the gold, they say nothing about it.

The goldsmith gets his half-rupee, and packs up his tools, and marches away, to find some more customers.

A LITTLE ABOUT CASTE.

THE Hindoo goldsmith belongs to a caste called Sudra. This is the lowest of the four great castes or classes of people in India. The highest caste of all, is the caste of the Brahmin.

The Brahmins are the priests of the Hindoos. They are supposed to pass their lives in study, and in thinking about holy things. The second caste includes the soldiers and people who have to do with matters of state. The third caste includes the merchants and farmers.

And last of all comes the fourth caste, which includes the poor Sudra.

The Sudras are labourers, and work with their hands. They are goldsmiths, and tailors, and so on.

There is a foolish story which the Brahmins tell about the four castes.

They say, that when mankind was created, the priests came from the mouth of the god Brahma. The soldiers came out of his arms. The merchants came out of his breast. And the Sudras came out of his foot.

The Brahmin is, in point of rank, the highest person in the land. He walks about with a white cord round his neck, and expects every one to do him homage. But he is not always rich. There are so many Brahmins, that some of them must be poor. But it does not make them any the less proud.

A LITTLE ABOUT CASTE.

The Sudra will often be rich, but he is always looked down upon. The Brahmin will hardly deign to speak to him, or look at him. But he holds the Brahmin in great reverence, and will do anything to please him. He will wait upon him, and chop wood, and fetch water, and work like a slave.

What does the Brahmin do in return? He will hold out his hand a little way; and this he calls giving the Sudra a blessing.

Sometimes the Brahmin will get so poor, and the Sudra so rich, that the Brahmin will be cook in the kitchen of the Sudra. But even here, he will strut about, and give himself airs, and quite look down upon his master. The three first castes regard themselves as far above the Sudra.

"I AM HOLIER THAN THOU!"

The Sudra cannot choose a wife from any of them. But the other castes can marry among the Sudras if they like.

There are a number of smaller castes besides these four great ones.

The lowest caste of all includes the Pariahs or outcasts.

They are treated like dogs. Even the Sudra will not touch them with his garment, lest he should be defiled.

A man would lose caste if he touched a Pariah.

The man in the picture is cooking his dinner of rice. He is sadly afraid the other man should come near him, because he is of a lower caste.

He might be saying, "Stand by, for I am holier than thou."

The missionaries in India are trying to get rid of caste. They teach the people that God has made "of one blood all nations, to dwell on the face of the earth," and that our Saviour gave His life a ransom for all. The despised Pariah is as precious in His eyes as the Brahmin. If a Hindoo becomes a Christian, of course he loses caste at once. This is almost as bad as losing his life.

His nearest friends, even his wife and children, hate and persecute him. He will be driven out of society, and none of his own people will speak to him, or allow him to come near them.

GOING TO SCHOOL IN INDIA.

When a Hindoo boy is about five years old, his father will send him to the village school.

What kind of a school is it?

It is often held out of doors. The boys sit under the shade of the beautiful palm-trees.

They sit cross-legged on the skin of a tiger, or an antelope; or else they have a mat made of palm-leaves. They begin school very early in the morning, before the sun gets hot.

No one can do anything in the hottest part of the day, and the school is shut up.

The boy is taught his letters first. He is made to write them with his finger on the ground. When he begins to improve, he writes them on a palm-leaf. The palm-leaf is his slate, and a reed, or a short rod of iron, with a sharp point, is his pencil.

The sharp-pointed iron is called a stylus. Twice a day, the boys stand up and say their lessons. If they are idle they are punished.

The schoolmaster sits on the ground, with his pupils before him. He is a very grave-looking man, and is either a Brahmin or a Sudra.

HINDOO CHILDREN AT A MISSIONARY SCHOOL.

He gets very little for his teaching. When a boy first comes to school he pays a penny a month. But when he can write he pays twopence, and so on. The higher he rises in the school, the more money he pays.

What is the boy taught?

He is taught the prayers to the gods, which he learns by heart. If he wants to be a scholar, and can afford to pay his teachers, he can learn the different dialects in India, and as much other knowledge as his teacher can give him.

When the boy is about nine years old, he is let to join the caste of the Brahmins.

That is, if his parents belong to that caste.

Till he does this, he is only looked upon as a Sudra.

Sometimes, while he is still quite a child, he will set off and go on a pilgrimage. Often a boy, who goes in this way, never comes back any more.

When a boy becomes a Brahmin he has the sacred cord given to him to wear. It is made of three thick twists of cotton; each twist is intended to represent one of the three gods.

Brahma, Vishnu, and Siva.

The cotton, of which this cord is made, must only be touched by the hands of the Brahmins.

The Brahmins gather it from the plant, and spin and twist it, and in fact make it into the cord.

There are so many rites to be observed, and so many people to be feasted, that it is rather expensive to invest a boy with the sacred cord. Some of the poorer Brahmins cannot afford it, and they have to beg money of their richer neighbours.

A great feast is provided, of rice, and fruit, and butter, and cocoa, and many other kinds of food. And everything must be cooked in a new vessel, bought for the occasion, and which has never been near the fire. Not one of these new cooking vessels may ever be used again.

The boy is made to sit on a stool and is anointed with oil, and a new garment put upon him. A string of coral beads is hung round his neck, and bracelets are put on his arms. And, to finish his toilette, the edges of his eyelids are stained with black.

His father and mother now sit down beside him, and the women come and sing hymns and songs, wishing him all kinds of happiness.

There are a great many tedious rites, and there is a great deal of feasting and singing. Indeed, it is several days before the ceremony is over.

The best kind of school in India is that you see in the picture. It is a missionary school.

Here a number of poor little Hindoos are taught to read the Bible. The missionaries are their teachers.

They have left their own homes in England, and come all the way to India on purpose.

The more children are taught in these schools the better. Let us hope they may grow up Christians instead of poor ignorant heathens, bowing down to idols of wood and stone.

HOUSES IN INDIA.

WHAT kind of houses have the people in India?

The poor people have not very good houses. Indeed, they are mere huts, and have but one room. The walls are made of a frame-work of bamboo, with straw matting inside. Outside, they are plastered with mud.

The roof of the hut is thatched.

There is a thick hedge often found before a row of huts or cottages. And often a beautiful clump of palms will screen the dwellings from sight.

The better class of people live in brick houses. The houses are built round a court, and have a verandah inside the court.

The poor man has not much furniture in his house. He has a mat on the floor. He will sit on it, or sleep on it, or have his dinner set upon it. He has no chair, or table, or bed; nothing but his mat.

He has a basin, made of clay, to hold his rice. His lamp is made of the shell of the cocoa-nut. He has a wooden spoon, and a couple of stones to use as a pestle and mortar. His plates and dishes are of leaves.

This is about all.

Even the rich people do not care to have their rooms full of furniture, unless they wish to imitate the English. Then, they cram their rooms so full of English furniture, that you can hardly move.

There are no carpets on the floors. The smooth polished floor does not want one. A white cloth is spread on it. There are cushions for people to recline upon. A great fan hangs from the ceiling, and is called a punkah. This fan is pulled by a string, and made to move backwards and forwards to cool the air.

Everything is done in India to keep the rooms cool.

All the rooms open into the verandah, and instead of windows, matting made of bamboo, is hung down. The servants keep throwing water on the matting, to cool the air as it comes in.

At night, muslin curtains are drawn tightly round the bed, to keep out the mosquitoes.

As soon as the sun goes down it is dark. There is no twilight as there is in England.

When it is dark, crowds of insects fly into the houses if they can, and flicker about the lamps. Sometimes, the crowd of insects will be so great as to put the lamps out.

THE SACRED RIVER.

THE Hindoos spend a great deal of their time and strength in going pilgrimages.

Where do they go to ?

To a great many places, which are called sacred places.

There are some towns, on the river Ganges, which are thought sacred.

The river Ganges flows, as you will see by looking at the map, through a great part of India.

It is looked upon as a sacred stream, and people come from all parts of the country to bathe in its waters.

The poor Hindoo thinks the water will wash away his sin. And if he dies in the river, he feels quite sure he will go to heaven.

Why is the Ganges thought to be holy ?

The reason the Brahmins give is this.

They say, that once the wife of Siva put her hands, in play, before the eyes of her husband.

Siva is one of the Hindoo gods.

The world went wrong, because, for a few moments, Siva was blindfold; and he was said to be in such distress, that drops fell from his forehead.

These drops were the source from which the river Ganges began to flow.

There are other rivers in India which are sacred, and to which pilgrims go.

When the pilgrim cannot go to the river, he has a contrivance by which he can make the river come to him.

A number of men employ themselves in filling jars with water from the Ganges, or some other river. Then, they put their jars in baskets. The baskets are fastened one to each end of a pole, and are carried over the man's shoulder.

It is thought a great indignity to carry a burden on the head. Only the poorer classes of Hindoos ever do it.

How does the man use the water?

He sells it sometimes; and the further he gets from the river, the better price he can ask for it.

If he is a religious beggar, as many of the Brahmins are, he will give it away for nothing.

A great deal of the water is used in the temples of the idols. The priest throws it over the idol.

But some of the water-carriers are as cunning as the jugglers. They are often suspected of getting the water out of the nearest river they can find, or even out of a ditch.

In the picture, a water-carrier is washing his jars and pots in the river. Behind him is an idol temple.

The time of year when the pilgrims set off for their pilgrimage is the cool season. I cannot call it winter, for it is never winter in the torrid zone.

Then the roads are thronged with persons, all wending their way to one sacred spot or other.

Some trudge along on foot, carrying baskets of provisions, slung over their shoulders.

These baskets will be adorned with peacock's feathers. For the peacock is a very common bird in India.

Here, and there, a man will trot along on a pony, or drive a rude kind of cart—with jingling bells to the horse's head. And you will see a rich Brahmin strutting along under a screen or canopy —gay with peacocks' feathers, and with little bells hung inside.

Sometimes a child will mix with the crowd, carrying a lamb or a kid in its arms.

And a poor old man will totter along, supported, perhaps, by his sons. He knows he has not long to live, and he wishes to die on the banks of the sacred river.

Yonder, too, is a lame man, who has hard work to struggle on. He means to throw aside his crutches, and plunge into the river.

Will he be drowned?

Yes. But he thinks his soul will go straight to heaven!

THE SACRED RIVER.

BENARES.

THE most sacred city in India is called Benares.

The Brahmins think it is so sacred, that if a man lives in it only a little time, he is sure to go to heaven.

I think you will be quite shocked at all the foolish things the Brahmins say!

Benares stands upon rather high ground, and looks over the broad

THE SACRED CITY OF BENARES.

stream of the Ganges. There are temples built all down to the water's edge. The whole city is full of temples.

Benares looks very grand at a distance, with all its temples and buildings. But, if you come nearer, you will see that the streets are very narrow indeed. A man on horseback can scarcely get down them in some places.

BENARES.

ZEBU, OR SACRED BULL OF INDIA.

The houses on the opposite sides of the street nearly touch each other.

Sometimes there will be a gallery across from one to the other.

Here, and there, are poor tumble-down cottages, covered with dust and spiders' webs.

The web has been spun by a very great spider, which lives in India.

The web is as thick as gauze or muslin, and looks like curtains hanging from the wall.

These ruinous places have the walls covered with pictures. You can see them still. There is the elephant, the monkey, the camel, and the peacock.

Some of the temples are covered with beautiful carvings of animals, and flowers, and branches of palms.

The Hindoos love to have their buildings all over pictures and carvings. And they use red paint, which often looks very staring and gaudy.

Besides the people who crowd the narrow streets, you meet with numbers of animals.

There are the sacred bulls.

They are white, with a hump on their shoulders, and are as tame as possible. No one would think of hurting them, for they are looked upon as holy. So they go about, putting their noses into the doors of the shops or houses, to ask for something nice to eat; or they will lie asleep across the street, taking up every bit of the room.

It is not very easy to make them get up, for it is thought a sin to strike them, and they are very lazy.

Some of the bulls do a little work. But the people treat them with great respect, and would not kill one on any account.

Besides the bulls, there are the sacred monkeys. The island of Ceylon was said to have been conquered by a god in the shape of a monkey. So the monkeys of Benares lead just as easy a life as the bulls.

There are crowds of them in some parts of the town. They scramble on the roofs of the temples, and cling to the projecting parts, as they do to the trees in their native forests.

If they kept on the roofs, all would be well. But they pop their heads into the shops, where fruit and sweetmeats are sold, and snatch what comes in their way. If a child is going down the street, with its dinner in its hand, a monkey is very likely to start up and snatch it away.

In fact, there is no end to the mischief and robbery of the monkeys.

THE MAN DROWNING HIMSELF IN THE RIVER GANGES.

WHEN a pilgrim comes to the Ganges, he sits down on the edge of the river, and has his head shaved.

He contrives that every hair shall fall into the sacred stream.

THE MAN DROWNING HIMSELF IN THE RIVER GANGES.

For every hair, that is touched by the water, he thinks he shall enjoy a million years in Paradise!

In some places, the Ganges is considered to be more holy than in others.

There is a poor little town on the banks of the river, just where it comes from the mountains to flow into the plains of India.

The town has not more than a thousand houses in it, but the Hindoos regard it with great reverence.

The crowd of pilgrims has been known to number a million and a half.

When this mighty host have assembled, they draw up, and wait till the favourable moment for rushing into the water.

A Brahmin gives the signal. He is supposed to know when it will be proper.

Then, down rush the poor devoted pilgrims, struggling and fighting with each other, which shall get into the river first.

The street leading to the river is very narrow; once, the rush was so terrible, and the crushing and struggling so great, that many people were squeezed to death.

Since then, the street has been made wider, on purpose to prevent such an accident from happening any more.

But nothing can prevent the poor foolish people from throwing away their lives.

A man will walk into the river, with a great jar tied on each side of his waist. The jars will keep him from sinking, as long as they are empty. But what do you think he does?

He has a cup in his hand, and he begins to fill the jars, till they get heavy and drag him down under the water. All the time, the Brahmins on the bank keep shouting to him, and telling him he will go to heaven.

And so the poor deluded man sinks deeper and deeper, and at last is drowned!

THE BRAHMINS' KINDNESS TO DUMB ANIMALS.

THERE is one doctrine that the Brahmins teach, which is called by a very long name.

It is called the transmigration of souls.

What does it mean?

It means that when a man dies, his soul passes into some other body; perhaps the body of an animal, or a bird, or even an insect.

We know this cannot be true, and it is a very foolish doctrine indeed.

But it makes the Brahmins afraid of killing anything. A Brahmin has been known to wear a piece of gauze over his mouth, lest he should draw any fly or insect into his mouth, and swallow it.

There is a hospital at a place called Surat.

The hospital is a large piece of ground, with high walls round it. The patients are taken the greatest care of. But they are not men and women. They are all animals!

If a dog or a horse were to get old, and not be able to do any more work, it would be taken to the hospital, and kept there all the rest of its life.

Or if an animal gets hurt, it can go to the hospital and be doctored. Of course, the hospital is full of all kinds of creatures.

There are horses, and mules, and sheep, and goats, and monkeys; and I cannot tell you what else besides.

Some of the better sort of Brahmins say that the hospital has been founded merely out of kindness to animals.

But the very same Brahmins who think so much of dumb animals, would rather die than eat with a poor Sudra. They would think they were defiled by the Sudra, and would be afraid of losing caste.

As for the Pariahs, a Brahmin would not touch one of them with his little finger.

A boat full of Pariahs was once upset on the river.

All the Pariahs went to the bottom, and were drowned; because not one of the Brahmins would stretch out his hand to help them!

THE TIGER OF THE JUNGLE.

THE middle part of Hindostan is one great plain.

But it is not like the great plains we have been talking about; such as the Pampas, or the Prairie.

The Plains of India, as they are called, are as rich and as fertile as any part of the world.

Great rivers wind through them, and water them. The land has been cultivated as carefully as it is in England. All kinds of useful plants have been reared by the English, and shipped off to other countries.

Rice, and sugar, and indigo, and cotton, and opium, are sent out from India.

England has possession of nearly the whole of Hindostan.

But there are parts of the rich plains of India that cannot be cultivated.

The trees, and shrubs, and bushes have grown so thick and matted together, that no axe can make a way through them. Miles and miles of ground are covered with jungle.

A body of armed men could not force their way through the jungle. Trees spread their giant arms on every side. Tall canes shoot up, in a few months, to the height of sixty feet. Prickly shrubs and thorny bushes fill up every space. And there is the jungle grass itself, which is taller than a man. It is very soft and silky to look at, but a man would soon be lost if he tried to make a path through it.

Have I given you any idea of what the jungle is?

The English have stations all over India, where soldiers live, on purpose to keep the country in order.

Some of these stations are called jungle-stations, because they are near to the jungle.

The soldiers, and the people who live there, see a great deal of the tiger. In India he is called the Royal Tiger. A company of English merchants used to pay a pound for every tiger that was killed.

THE TIGER OF THE JUNGLE.

Even now, when the soldiers are marching, a tiger will sometimes spring out of the jungle, with a great roar, and carry off a man in his mouth.

The jungle is his favourite lurking-place. When he is very hungry he will come out, and go prowling close to the houses. He will even break into the stable, and carry off a horse.

You may think how much he is dreaded. People hunt him, and do all they can to get rid of him. Tiger-hunting is a grand sport in India.

But the tiger sometimes meets with an enemy in the depths of his own jungle, and when he is out of the reach of man.

TIGER AND SNAKE.

There are bright-coloured snakes gliding about amongst the dead leaves, or else twisting themselves round the trees.

In the picture, the tiger has laid himself down to sleep. The bones of some poor creature he has devoured are beside him. Close over his head is the snake hanging from a branch. He darts his poisoned fangs into the neck of the tiger.

The tiger starts up, and roars, and howls, and is in a great rage.

But in a very short time, the poison spreads all over his body, and he dies.

THE BUNGALOW IN THE JUNGLE.

THE people in the jungle-station live in bungalows.

What is a bungalow?

A bungalow is a country house, or villa. It is built of unbaked mud, and the roof is either thatched or tiled.

The rooms open into a verandah, and there is a lattice-work of bamboo to fit into the doorways.

The doors have often to be left open all night, because of the heat.

If it were not for the lattice-work, wolves and hyenas would walk straight in. They prowl about in the verandah, and make a dismal howling.

The thatch of the bungalow is a famous place for wild cats to hide in. They are, of course, hidden from sight, for they cannot get through the ceiling. Sometimes a cloth, stretched over the top of the room, is the only ceiling.

But the cats can be heard scratching and fighting, and a famous noise they make.

The noise of the cats is not the only one. There is the croaking of enormous toads and frogs, and the chirping of crickets. The crickets chirp twice as loud as they do in England.

And there will be loud yells from the troop of jackals who are roaming about in the distance.

Each animal seems as if it were trying to make more noise than its neighbour.

Can the people get any sleep?

They try to do, for they are pretty well used to noises. Their beds are very high, and are in the middle of the room. They are raised up, for fear of the insects that might be on the floor.

And the beds have muslin curtains, tightly tucked in, all round them.

This is done to keep out some troublesome flies, called mosquitoes, and a crowd of other insects besides.

You have to be very quick to be a match for the insects.

You have to jump into bed, and draw the curtains tight in a moment.

The mosquitoes are all on the watch.

If only one contrived to get in, you would soon be roused by a sharp bite on the face.

And till you got up and killed it, there would be no chance of any more sleep.

THINGS TO BE SEEN IN THE JUNGLE.

PEOPLE who live near the jungle, see a great many beautiful things.

Green pigeons, and little brown doves with pink breasts, come flying in flocks.

There are sparrows with bright yellow breasts, that look, as they fly all together, like a cloud of gold.

To say nothing of the humming-birds, and sun-birds, that flash about here and there like so many gems.

Crowds of gaily-dressed parrots lead a very happy life among the trees of the jungle.

They crack the stones of the different fruits that grow on every side, and pick out the kernels.

Then, they fly to some stream or river to take a bath, and splash about at the edge of the water, and scream and chatter like so many children at play.

In the heat of the day, they are still enough. They go to sleep in some cool shady place among the branches.

The branches of the tree will be crowded with parrots, but not a sound will be heard. They are all fast asleep.

There are great holes in the trunks of some of the trees, and here

PARROTS.

the parrots make their sleeping-rooms. When night comes, they creep in, and are as snug as possible.

THINGS TO BE SEEN IN THE JUNGLE.

There is another bird in the jungle, that you have seen a great many times.

I mean the peacock.

This hot country is his home. In every glade and open space he may

THE PEACOCK.

be seen spreading out his splendid plumes, and strutting about as he does in England.

He roosts in the top of the tall trees. One tree will sometimes have as many as a dozen peacocks upon it.

Do you see the nest in the picture? It belongs to a bird called the tailor-bird.

She was so anxious to hide her nest from the snakes and monkeys, that she fastened it to a leaf.

She picked up a dead leaf, and sewed it to the underside of the living one.

In the space between, she made a snug little nest, and lined it with gossamer. The tiny nest swings about, as the leaf moves, with the wind. You could not see that it was there, unless you looked very closely.

When the little tailor-birds are hungry, they put out their heads to see if

TAILOR-BIRD.

their mother is coming. But if a noise frightens them, they draw them in, and nothing is to be seen but the leaf swinging in the wind.

The tailor-bird is a tiny creature, and is about the size of the humming-bird.

She has a long slender bill, that she uses for a needle. The fibres of a plant she uses for her thread.

You see how neatly she has sewed the two leaves together.

Is there anything else to be seen in the jungle?

Oh yes! Large butterflies, dressed in scarlet and yellow, and blue and purple, and I cannot tell you how many colours besides, flutter about the flowers.

Huge winged grasshoppers, such as we never see in England, with bodies of the most vivid green, hop about among the grass. And there are beetles, decked with such glowing colours, that they look like precious stones.

When it is dark, the fireflies flit about among the trees. It seems as if hundreds of fairies were carrying about tiny torches in their hands.

THE WET SEASON AND THE DRY.

In India, there can scarcely be said to be either spring or summer, autumn or winter.

There are but two seasons—the rainy season and the dry season.

The dry season begins about the end of October, and lasts till April. All this time, there is not a drop of rain, scarcely even a cloud to sail across the sky.

The sun pours down its burning rays day after day, and by degrees every plant and blade of grass is burnt up. Except in the forests and the jungles, the whole country looks brown and bare as a road. The earth cracks for very dryness, and there are chasms several feet in depth.

It is not very pleasant to travel in the dry season. The heat of the dry parched road is scarcely to be borne. And great clouds of dust are blown up by the wind, and are almost as bad as the sand storms of the desert.

If it were not for the great rains, India would be a land of famine and of death.

But the people know that the dry weather will come to an end, at the appointed time. The sky begins to look cloudy, and there will come fierce

THE WET SEASON AND THE DRY.

blasts of wind, such as we have no idea of in England. There will be flashes of lightning, that light up the whole sky, and keep on, flash after flash, for hours. All the time, the thunder never ceases to roll, either in the distance, or with a dreadful crash as the storm comes nearer.

The rain will pour down in torrents, as if the windows of heaven had been opened.

People, from their houses, can see the whole country become like a flood. The rivers overflow, and every little brook is swelled to a stream.

Sometimes the huts of the natives will be swept away.

A thick fog hangs all over the country, that the sun cannot pierce. This keeps falling in incessant torrents of rain.

HOUSES SWEPT AWAY BY THE FLOODS.

The rain soon turns the desert land into a fruitful plain.

But the climate of India is not all alike. In some parts of the country, the rainy weather lasts for eight months of the year; and in Bengal, there are changes very much like England—from rain to fine, and from a clear sky to a fog.

Up in the mountains the weather is as cold as can be; and the higher you get the colder it will be. By moving about, the people in India can have whatever climate they like.

BRIDGES IN INDIA.

You would not like to cross some of the bridges in India. Up in the mountains the rivers and torrents have bridges over them that make you turn giddy to look at.

AN INDIAN BRIDGE.

In one place, the trunk of a tree is thrown across the river. It is made a little flat in the middle, so that people can walk upon it. And at each end it is made fast to the young stem of a tree.

Over this bridge, men, women, and animals have to pass.

The poor animals do not always get over safely. Sometimes the weight of too many at once, pushes the bridge out of its place. The stem, that holds it on one side, gives way, and the bridge will be tilted up in a very dangerous manner. Often a goat will be pushed into the stream, and be drowned.

In another place, where the river is not very wide, there is a bridge made of rope.

There are two or three ropes, fastened to strong stakes driven down into each bank of the river, and about eight feet above the water.

The person, who is going to cross, takes fast hold of the ropes, and hangs by them. There is a little hoop, like a ring, that runs up and down the rope. The man can sit in this hoop if he likes. He goes, pushing himself along by his hands, till he gets to the opposite bank. Sometimes, if he is rather nervous, and thinks he shall fall, people help him across.

They blindfold his eyes, that he may not see the water rushing and foaming beneath. Then, they tie his hands and feet to the ropes, and pull him over by a rope tied round his waist.

A great many tribes of people live up in the mountains, and they are used to these bridges.

In one place, there is no bridge at all over the river.

How do people get across?

They wait till they have collected a great many gourds. These gourds or pumpkins are very large indeed, and are fastened in a string, and tied round the waist of the native who is acting as guide.

The great pumpkins hold the man up in the water, so that he is in no danger of sinking. Then, the person who is going to cross, takes fast hold of the guide, and is safely floated to the other side.

The guides carry the luggage of the travellers on their heads, and swim over the river, held up by the gourds.

THE STORY OF JUGGERNAUT.

THERE is one place where the castes of India meet together.

At the temple of the god Juggernaut.

People who are on board a ship in the Bay of Bengal, can see in the distance a great building like a pyramid. The top of the pyramid is adorned with a number of copper balls, which glisten and flash in the sun.

THE STORY OF JUGGERNAUT.

This is the temple of Juggernaut.

Who is Juggernaut?

Juggernaut is a frightful idol, that the Hindoos have worshipped for many hundreds of years.

The temple stands by the sea-side, in a province of India called Orissa.

It stands in the middle of a great sandy plain. There is not a blade of grass to be seen near it.

There are a great many temples; but the largest of all is the temple where the idol is kept. There are two other idols in the same temple. They are called his brother and sister.

What are the idols like?

They are three monstrous wooden dolls, with their faces painted, black, and white, and yellow. Their bodies are rough blocks of wood, with wrappers of cloth round them.

There are two great feasts in honour of Juggernaut.

At one of these feasts, the idols are brought out and showed to the people.

The idols are set on a terrace in front of the temple, and hundreds and thousands of pilgrims stand to look at them.

A canopy of red cloth is over the head of the idols, and the Brahmins stand by them, and keep fanning them, lest the flies should settle on their faces. The multitude of fans almost prevents the idols from being seen.

But the grandest of the feasts is called the feast of the chariot.

Juggernaut and the two other idols are taken out for a ride. Then, the huge car of Juggernaut is brought up to the temple.

You have no doubt read about this dreadful car, a great many times.

The Brahmins drag the three huge idols to their cars. They tie a cord round their necks, and some of the Brahmins pull, and some push behind. The three great dolls go rocking and pitching through the crowd to get to their cars.

When the people see Juggernaut, they give a tremendous shout, and cry, "Victory to Juggernaut!"

What is the car like?

It is a little like a pagoda, with a pointed roof, covered with spangled cloth, and a flag at the top.

It is forty feet high, and runs upon heavy wooden wheels.

When the signal has been given, the immense crowd press round the car, and seize on the ropes that hang to it. Bands of music begin to play, and amidst a tumult of shouts, and cheers, that are quite deafening, the car begins to move.

CAR OF JUGGERNAUT.

It goes creaking and rumbling along, through the crowd, dragged by the people.

Now and then, a pilgrim lies down in front of the car, and lets the wheels go over him.

Then, the people shout and cheer still louder, and throw flowers upon his body.

You will be glad to hear, that the English soldiers prevent the pilgrims from throwing away their lives in this shocking manner. And I do not think they will allow the car of Juggernaut to be dragged out any more.

Let us hope that the knowledge of the true God will spread into this dark land, and that the Sun of righteousness may rise on the poor Hindoo, with healing in His beams.

THE GREAT BAT OF JAVA.

The banian tree, with its hundreds of spreading branches, gives shelter to man and animals.

The beautiful green pigeon feeds and lives among its branches. And another creature, of a very different species from the pigeon, makes its home there.

I mean the giant bat of Java.

This bat is so large, that when its wings are spread, they measure six feet from the tip of one wing to that of the other.

Thousands of these monstrous creatures shelter in the banian tree all day.

They hang from the branches by their claws, or else by the hook that is on their wings. They hang with their heads downwards, fast asleep.

If any one disturbs them, they utter sharp shrill cries, and begin to struggle in a very awkward manner. Their claws are so sharp, and take such fast hold of the tree, that they cannot all in a moment get loose.

When evening comes, the bat wakes up, and begins to feel hungry. He unlooses himself from the branch, and flies out, flapping his great leathern wings.

Thousands of bats fly out at the same time, like a cloud. The mother bat will have her little one sticking to her breast.

What does the bat eat?

Insects, and little birds, and mice, and rats. But he has a great liking for ripe fruit. He is almost sure to go off to some garden and rob it.

THE ORANG-OUTANG IN TROUBLE.

The bats settle on the trees, and eat as much fruit as they can. The poor man's garden is robbed as well as the rich man's. All suffer alike from the midnight feasts of the bats.

The owner of the garden often takes his revenge.

In the clear moonlight, he can see the bats coming. They fly with a slow steady pace, and in a straight line. He knows they are making for his fruit trees.

He loads his gun, and takes his stand.

On come the huge bats, not all at once. First one bat arrives, and another follows him at a little distance.

But before the first bat has reached the tree, there is a sharp report, and a rattling sound.

Down will drop the great bat, shot, perhaps, through the head.

THE WILD MAN OF THE WOODS.

Did you ever see an orang-outang?

He is sometimes called the wild man of the woods.

He is not a man at all. He is only a monkey.

Once he used to live in India, but the race has died out. He is found in the dense forests of Sumatra, an island which lies very near to India.

The orang-outang likes the deep dark forest. Like all the monkeys, his arms are very strong, and he swings himself from branch to branch, and gets along as fast as a horse can gallop.

In the daytime, he lives very much on the tops of the trees. He is looking out for his food.

He will eat the young tender shoots, and the leaves, and the fruit. He does not eat anything else. At night, he hides himself snugly in the thick boughs and leaves.

Sometimes he makes a bed for himself by weaving the boughs together. Then he will lie down and go fast asleep.

In the picture the poor orang is in sad trouble.

The people, who live in the island, are fond of roast monkey, and think the flesh of the orang is a very great dainty. You see they have come out with bows and arrows to shoot him.

The orang tries to get out of their way. He climbs up a tree, and goes on swinging himself from one tree to another.

The hunters follow him up, and keep shooting arrows. At last, the orang gets into a passion, and begins to break the boughs, and throw them to the ground. The more boughs he breaks, the worse it is for him.

The hunters can now see him quite plainly. Indeed, they will wait until he has broken off all the friendly twigs and boughs that would have hidden him.

Then their arrows fly faster, and with more effect. The poor orang soon falls to the ground, and is killed.

The Indians can feast on roast monkey to their heart's content. And they can make caps and helmets of his skin, to be worn on high days and holidays.

THE RAINLESS DESERT.

The desert is not at all like the steppes, or the prairie, or any of the great plains I have been telling you about.

In the steppes the ground is dry, and bare and scorched in summer. But in winter there will be rain and snow. The ground will be flooded. Then grass springs up, and herbs and plants for the cattle.

But in the desert several years will pass without a drop of rain. It is called the rainless desert.

Even at night there is no cooling dew to drop on the ground.

There is neither rain nor dew.

You will not wonder that no green thing can grow. There is no grass to tread upon. You tread upon the hot burning sand. The fierce sun makes the sand so hot.

The soil is a thick layer of sand. Now and then, there will be a sandy

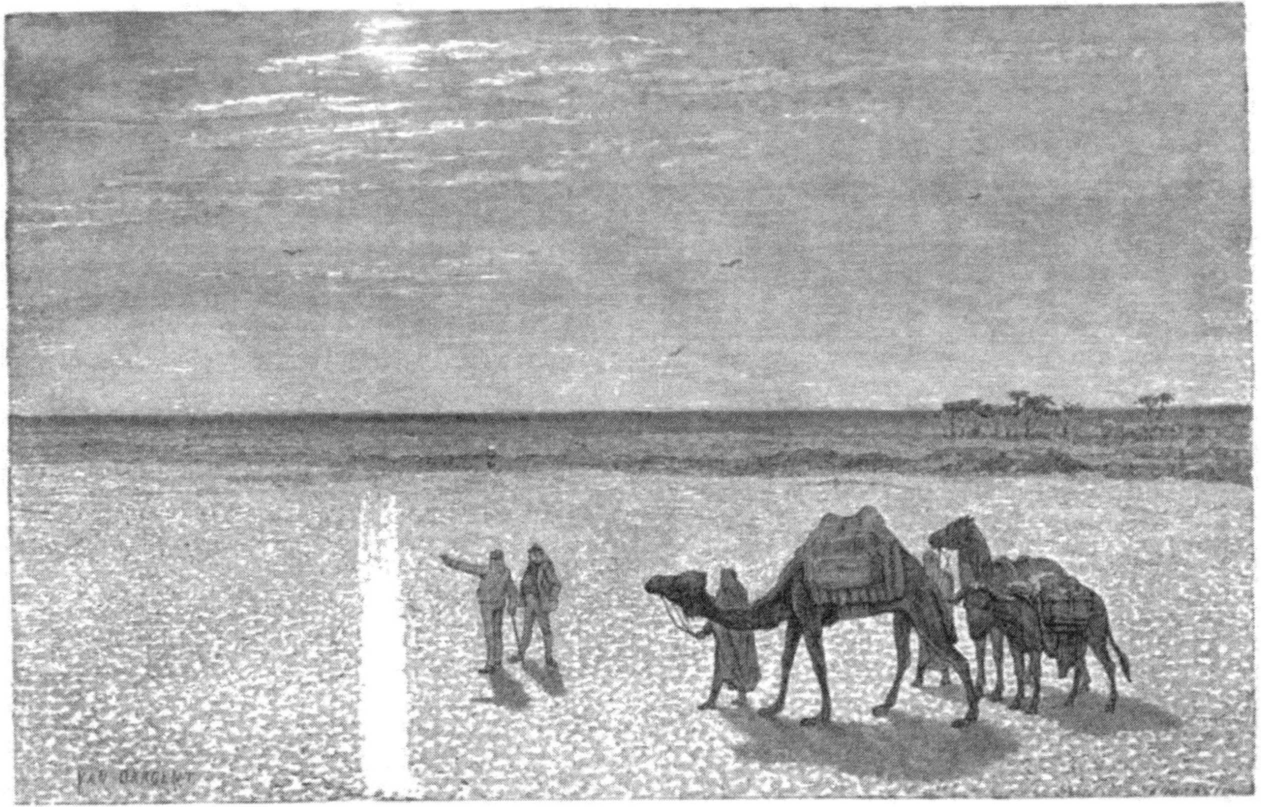

SALT LAKE.

rock, or a mass of broken stone. Underneath the sand is a bed of lime, which is full of salt.

There is one region of desert which is all salt. It is called a salt lake, though it is really a plain.

The salt is so firm and hard that a camel can tread upon it without sinking in. Sometimes a horse goes over it, and his iron shoes will break through the crust of salt. But he only sinks a very little way. There is another crust or layer of salt beneath, even harder than the first.

The plain is of such a brilliant whiteness that it almost dazzles you. Great pieces of salt lie on the ground, and glitter like crystals. The blue sky above looks black by contrast with the whiteness of the plain.

Where is the Salt Lake?

It is near the Isthmus of Suez, not far from the Mediterranean Sea.

The Arabs call this lake Baudouin, which means Baldwin.

The Crusaders gave it this name. Baldwin, Count of Flanders, was one of their leaders.

THE LION OF THE DESERT.

WHAT kind of animals live in the desert?

No animal lives in the desert of sand. It could find nothing to eat.

The desert of sand is a frightful solitude. There is silence, like that of the grave.

Where are these deserts of sand?

One is in Arabia. It is called the Desert of Arabia.

One is in Africa. It is called the great Desert of Sahara.

The Desert of Sahara has in it deep abysses of sand. Once, a king of Persia marched his army into it. He was going to cross it. But not one of his men was seen any more. The whole army was lost.

They either died of thirst, or were buried in some abyss of sand.

There are many bones of animals scattered about in the desert. The bones of camels and of poor travellers who have been lost.

But there are few living creatures to be met with.

Unless, indeed, the wild beasts follow on the track of the caravan, in hope of getting some prey.

Round about the desert, the country is very wild and dreary.

But rain falls now and then, and there are streams for the wild cattle to drink at. There is a rough kind of pasture, and there are trees and shrubs. It is a very different place from the desert of sand.

Here the wild beasts can prowl about, and find a home. The lion's roar is often heard in the night. You see him in the picture bringing food to the lioness and her cubs.

He is bringing them a gazelle.

He pounced upon it when it was asleep, or else so busy feeding that it did not see him. It can run so fast, and give such great bounds, that if it had seen him in time it might perhaps have escaped.

It is brave when it has a flock of companions round it.

Often another enemy will come stealing along. The spotted leopard is as fond of carrying off a gazelle as the lion is.

He comes crouching to the ground, and gliding along like a cat.

If the herd of gazelles see him coming, they do not run away. They stand close together, and butt at him with their long horns.

The leopard is very hungry indeed. But while they stand so firm he is likely to be disappointed.

He dare not run on their sharp horns, and he has to go away without his dinner.

THE WIND OF THE DESERT.

People who go through the desert have to face a great many discomforts.

One great enemy is the wind.

When the wind rises all in a moment, and begins to blow very hard indeed, you may fancy what happens.

It raises up the sand in a terrible manner. There is nothing to break

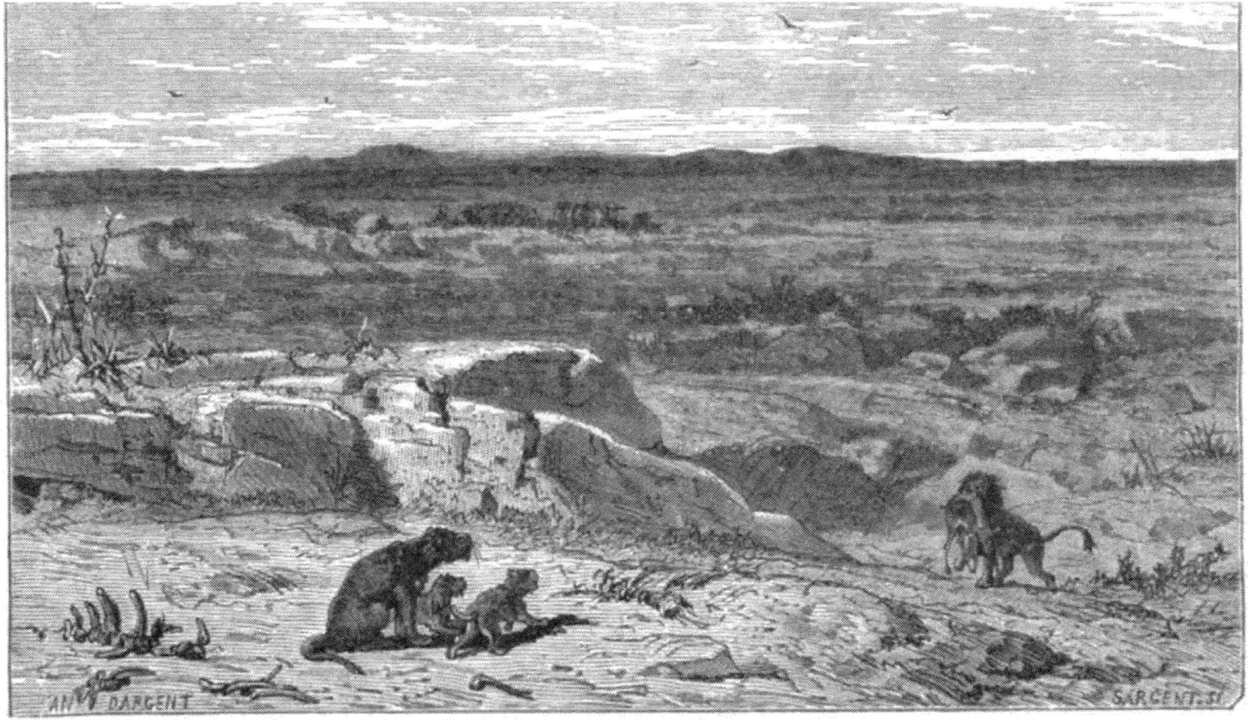
DARGENT
SARGENT. SC

LION OF THE DESERT.

THE WIND OF THE DESERT.

its fury. There are no houses, or hills, or trees. On it sweeps over the vast plain, the clouds of sand getting thicker every minute.

It grows dark, for the sun is hidden by the cloud of sand, and looks as pale as the moon.

What happens to the people who are caught in the storm?

They see it coming in the distance, and this is a very good thing.

THE SIMOOM.

There is a mist or haze in the horizon. The sky looks dim, and gusts of wind blow in their faces.

Not cool, pleasant wind. Oh no! The wind is so hot, that it might come from the mouth of a furnace.

The camel-drivers call out that the Khamsin is coming.

This is the name they give to this wind of the desert.

We call it the Simoom.

Then the people make haste, and get off their horses and their camels. They throw themselves on the ground, and wrap their heads up in their cloaks. There they lie as if they were dead, waiting for the simoom to come.

What happens to the camels?

The camels are pretty well used to the simoom. They know what to do. They kneel down, and poke with their noses into the sand. The camel has a way of shutting his nose tight up, so that the sand cannot get in.

On comes the simoom. You can hear the rushing of the mighty wind. The fine driving sand fills the whole air and sky. It is so hot, and so fine, that if it got down the throat it would scorch and suffocate.

Sometimes the sand covers over the men who are lying down, and half buries them. Then they move a little, and try to shake it off; but on no account will they uncover their faces.

If the simoom goes on blowing for a long time, it will dry up the water which the travellers are carrying in their water-skins.

When it has passed by, they all get up.

They feel very hot and uncomfortable, and their skin is dry and burning. But if they have taken care to keep their heads well wrapped up, they will not really be hurt by the simoom.

THE SAND THAT LOOKS LIKE WATER.

THERE is very little water in the desert.

Often, the travellers who are going across, get very thirsty indeed. Even the camels use up all the water in their pouches, and begin to want more.

They go on, stretching their long necks from side to side, and trying to smell water.

They can smell water a long way off.

THE SAND THAT LOOKS LIKE WATER.

By degrees, there appears in sight something that looks like a beautiful clear lake. How fresh and cool it is!

And a city must be close by, for there are temples and domes, and trees, all reflected in the lake.

Even the poor camels quicken their pace, and stretch out their necks. As for the travellers, the welcome word, "Water," goes from mouth to mouth.

But the Arab guide knows better. He wonders that his camels should be so taken in.

It is not water. It is the mirage.

If the poor travellers went up to it, they would find nothing but sand.

The fine temples, and the trees, and the cool lake, would all vanish away!

THE SAND THAT LOOKS LIKE WATER.

They were not *real*. They only looked like water.

What makes the mirage?

The effect of the sun on the glowing sand often makes it look like water.

And the piece of rock, or stone, or whatever lies near, is magnified into a tree or a temple. And more than that, the heat and thirst and fatigue affects the sight of the poor traveller in the desert. He cannot see clearly. Things seem to dance before his eyes.

You may think how disappointed he feels.

But the Arab guide has never expected anything. He is not disappointed.

He pushes on his camels until he reaches a spot where there is a real spring, or pool, and not sand that looks like water.

MEN OF THE DESERT.

Do you remember a story, in the Bible, about a boy who was driven into the wilderness? His mother was with him. Her name was Hagar.

Hagar was afraid her son would die by thirst. There was no water for him to drink. She laid him down on the ground, and went away that she might not see him die.

But he did not die. God had pity on the poor mother. And he caused a spring of water to gush out, so that the boy might drink.

Ishmael was the name of the boy.

He grew up, and became a kind of prince or chief. Just such a chief as an Arab chief is now.

The Arabs are descended from Ishmael.

You see what an ancient people they are.

There are a great many tribes of Arabs scattered about in Arabia, and the north of Africa.

The Arabs of the Desert are called Bedouins.

MEN OF THE DESERT.

They do not live in houses. They like to roam about in the free air of the desert. They may be called men of the desert.

Some of these Bedouins are shepherds, and keep flocks and herds. Besides this mode of living, they have another not so honest. They are apt to rob the caravans that pass through the desert.

BEDOUIN SHEPHERDS

From the time of the patriarch Job, the Arabs have been sad robbers.

If you remember, robbers fell on his cattle, and carried away all he had.

The Arabs have a curious way of robbing. If an Arab sees a man in the distance, he rides up to him, and says in a loud, shouting voice, "My mother is without a garment." This means that he wants to steal the garment of the traveller.

If the traveller gives it to him, the Arab will go quietly away. If he refuses, he is very likely to get killed.

People travel in caravans in order to be safe from the Arabs.

Many of the Bedouins do not keep flocks and herds. They have only one trade that of robbing.

These men are called children of the sword.

THE GREEN SPOT IN THE DESERT.

When the children of Israel journeyed through the wilderness, we are told that they set up their camp by some wells of water where palm-trees grew.

There is one palm which is called the Date Palm of the desert.

Its roots can take hold of the sandy soil, and draw nourishment from it.

The burning air and scorching sun do not hurt it. Its green glossy leaves throw a pleasant shadow. It is always lovely to look at; a thing that brings gladness to the heart.

Where palm-trees grow, and wells of water are found, and there is a green place in the desert, such a place is called an Oasis.

But you must not fancy an oasis to be merely a clump of trees and a little patch of verdure.

There are spots of verdure on the borders of the sandy desert.

Here and there, in hollow places, there will be a green sward, and a few stunted plants will grow.

The wandering Arab feeds his flocks on this pasture.

There are tribes of Arabs who lead more settled lives, and plant trees and gardens. These Arabs live in the oasis. An old writer once said that the great Desert of Sahara was like a leopard's skin, which has black spots on a yellow ground.

THE GREEN SPOT IN THE DESERT.

The yellow ground was the sand of the desert. The spots were the oases.

The oasis is almost covered with palm-trees.

A GREEN SPOT IN THE DESERT.

The Arab plants them in rows; and they are called palm-gardens.

He is more industrious than his wandering brother the Bedouin.

When there is no stream or rivulet, he sinks a well, and waters his palm-trees. All his riches are in the dates they will bear.

Their beautiful green leaves make a canopy, through which the sun cannot pierce.

He will plant also in his garden the fig, the pomegranate, and the apricot.

During the winter, he will grow turnips, and carrots, and onions, and such vegetables as we have in England.

The people live in houses of brick, with flat roofs and narrow windows.

They do not keep their streets and villages clean, as we do in England.

So that in spite of their lovely palm-gardens, and vines, and pomegranates, you would not like to live there.

The streets are full of heaps of rubbish, that lie there from week to week, and almost stop up the way.

Sometimes the wells, that the Arabs make, get choked up with sand. Then the palm-trees cannot be watered, and the villages become empty and desolate.

The fertile oasis gradually slips back to the desert.

THE ARAB'S TENT.

The Arabs of the desert move about from place to place, carrying their tents with them.

When they have found a place where there is a spring or well of water, and where grass grows, they encamp.

They stay until the grass is eaten up by their flocks, and then they go somewhere else.

An Arab tent is of a good large size. It is made of goats' hair, woven into a strong stuff.

The pieces of stuff are stitched together, and stretched on poles. There are a great many poles used to hold up a tent.

There are two rooms in the tent.

One is for the men, and one for the women.

A white woollen carpet hangs down between the rooms, and divides them from each other.

I daresay you would like to know what kind of rooms they are.

In the men's room, there is a carpet on the floor. In the middle of the floor, there will be a great heap of camel bags, and sacks of wheat. The great pile goes up nearly to the top of the tent.

The saddles of the camels serve instead of chairs and sofa.

The men sit on them and smoke.

The women's room has a great many things in it. For the women have most of the work to do.

There are the cooking materials. They are very simple. There are two copper pans. A mortar to pound the wheat in. A wooden bowl for the camels' milk. A wooden cup to drink out of; and a coffee pot.

ARABS AND THEIR TENTS.

When the dinner is going to be cooked, the largest of the copper pans is set over the fire, on three stones, which are kept on purpose.

Should you like to know what else is in the tent?

There is a curious thing like a cradle.

It is made of carpet, and covered with camel skin.

This is a saddle, on which the Arab women ride on the back of the camel.

A great many bits of coloured cloth are fastened to the saddle of the women. And there will be a few ostrich feathers. These flutter about in the wind as the camel marches along.

Then there is the stick to drive the camel with, and the little bells that hang round its neck. And there is a bag, to put the camel's hair in. For great tufts of hair keep falling off in the course of the journey.

And there are the water-skins. These are bags made of skin, and filled with water. The bag has a little side opening in it, to which the Arab can put his mouth and drink, as it hangs over the back of the camel.

The water-skins are very large, because the Arab takes as much water as he can, when he is going a journey.

Two skins are a load for a camel.

Then there is the leathern bucket, which brings up the water from the well. The Arab has no cord to let the bucket down with. He uses strips of leather twisted together.

All this leather comes from the skin of the camel.

The Arab has an iron chain that is very precious to him.

One end is fast to a ring that goes round the foot of his favourite horse.

The other end is made secure to an iron spike, and driven into the ground close by his bed.

So that it is not very easy to rob an Arab of his horse.

Has it ever been done?

Yes. A robber has come when the Arab is asleep, cut the chain, and carried off the horse without awaking its master.

FOOD OF THE ARABS.

IF a guest were to come to an Arab tent, the owner of the tent would set about to prepare him something to eat.

He would tell his wife to go to the flock, and choose out a lamb or a kid. Then it would be killed and dressed. The woman would boil it in camel's milk, and serve it in a large wooden dish.

Does not this remind you of the days of Abraham, when he told Sarah, his wife, to fetch a calf from the herd, and kill it, and dress it?

What do the Arabs live upon?

They make a paste of flour and water mixed together, and bake it in the ashes. Then they knead a little butter with it, and serve it up in a wooden bowl.

A little milk will be put in sometimes to make it nicer.

They have many dishes of this kind.

Rice and flour boiled with camel's milk is one dish. And bread, and butter, and dates, all mixed and kneaded together is another.

Have they any bread?

Yes; but it is unleavened. That is, there is no yeast in it. Little round cakes are baked on an iron plate. And they have a bread which they eat for breakfast, as we do hot rolls.

They scatter some stones on the ground, and make a brisk fire upon them. The dough is spread on the hot stones, and covered with glowing ashes. Then it is left till it is baked.

It is eaten hot; and is, in fact, hot bread.

The Arabs use the milk of the sheep and the goat to make butter.

DATE TREE.

The camel's milk is never taken for this purpose.

Shall I tell you how the Arab wife churns her butter?

She puts the milk into her great copper pan, and sets it over the fire. A little sour milk is added to it. After it has been on the fire a short time, she takes it off, and puts it into a bag of goat skin, and hangs it to one of the poles of the tent. For an hour or two, she keeps moving it backwards and forwards. She is churning her butter.

In due time, the butter comes. That is, the milk begins to thicken. Then she empties it out of the bag into a skin which is close by. And she gets more milk, and sets to work to churn again.

When she has churned a great deal of butter, she puts it all into the pan, and sets it over the fire. She throws in a handful of boiled wheat and a little yeast, which has been boiled with it, and then dried in the sun.

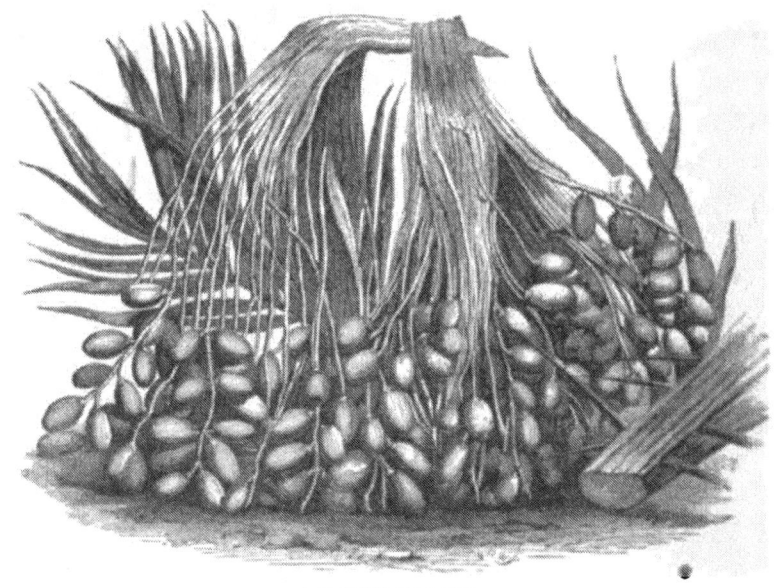

A CLUSTER OF DATES.

The butter in the pan boils for some time, and then it settles quite clear at the top. Under it is the butter-milk, which is drawn off and made very useful.

Sometimes it is beaten till it is thick, and then dried quite hard, and ground like flour in a mill.

There is a great deal of this ground butter-milk, and it is eaten mixed with the butter.

Do the Arabs make cheese?
Not often. They use all the milk for butter.
There is another dish which the Arabs think very nice.
It is made of truffles.
The truffle is a kind of fungus, which grows just under the ground.
People in some parts of England get truffles and sell them.
They are thought quite a dainty.
The Arab truffles will go on growing, till they come above ground. The camels will now and then stumble over them.
The Arab children dig them out of the ground with sticks. In the spring, each family will have several camel-loads of truffles.
While the stock of truffles lasts, the Arabs will live upon them, and save their other food.
They either boil or roast them. Or they make them into a paste with milk and water.
They are eaten with melted butter.
The truffles are sold in the markets for a halfpenny a pound.

ARABS AT DINNER.

As a rule, the Arab does not eat much meat.
His chief dish is flour mixed with camel's milk, and boiled.
The richest Arab in the tribe, never thinks of asking his wife to get him any better dinner.
When he has the chance, he will kill a gazelle. He dries its flesh in the sun, so that it will keep a long time.
Some tribes of Arabs live entirely on the dried flesh of the gazelles.
They have no flocks or herds, so they cannot have any milk.
Then the Arab likes to catch the jerboa.
What is the jerboa?
It is called the rat of the desert.

ARABS AT DINNER.

Its body is a little like a rat.

But its ears are large, and its tail very long indeed.

You see, in the picture, that it stands upright on its hind-legs, like a kangaroo.

THE JERBOA.

The Arab thinks the flesh of the jerboa a dainty morsel.

Now and then, the whole tribe has a grand feast.

A camel is killed.

This happens very seldom indeed.

Its flesh is cut up into large pieces. Part is boiled and part roasted. We should not think it nice at all.

Just before dinner, the Arab washes his hands.

There is a loose piece of the tent cloth, that flutters about in the wind. He uses it for a towel.

He eats his dinner very fast. The hot milk does not seem to scald his mouth.

If a guest is at table, he finds it hard work to keep pace with his host.

He will have to swallow his dinner boiling hot, or else go without it.

The Arab does not behave very well at meals. He will dip his hand into the dish, and take a great handful and swallow it.

After dinner, he does not wash his hands again. He licks the grease from his fingers, or else rubs them on the sheath of his sword.

The Arab women are not allowed to dine with the men. Any scraps are thought good enough for them to eat.

If a feast is being held in a tent, and the men go to it, their wives are never invited.

But the poor women do not like to be left at home fasting.

They steal after their husbands to the tent, and ask the hostess to give them a taste of something nice.

If she gives them a lamb's head or its foot, they are quite contented.

They think even that, better than nothing!

COFFEE.

THE drink the Arab likes the best is coffee.

What tea is to the Chinese, coffee is to the Arab.

The name of coffee comes from an Arabian word. And it is from Arabia that coffee was first brought.

It is now grown in many places besides. There are coffee plantations both in India and America.

Indeed, when people of every country began to drink coffee, Arabia could not supply it all.

The coffee you have for your breakfast was once a berry, and grew on a tree.

The tree had a stem about twelve feet high, and a number of slender branches that bent downwards.

Its flowers were white, and a little like those of the jessamine. When the flower was over, there came a red berry, something like a cherry.

The pulp of the berry had in it two hard seeds, about the size of a pea.

These were the coffee berries.

When the coffee trees are about three years old, they are in their prime.

COFFEE.

At the proper season, all the white blossoms come out at once, in a single night.

The trees look, the next morning, as if a shower of snow had fallen on them.

When the fruit is ripe, it falls from the tree. In Arabia, the owner of the coffee trees places cloths on the ground for the fruit to drop upon.

THE COFFEE PLANT.

Then the fruit is laid on mats, and well dried in the sun.

After this, the outer part, or dried pulp, is separated from the berries by washing.

There is still a hard covering, or rind, that wraps up the berry. This is removed by putting the berries through a wooden roller.

Next, the coffee has to be roasted.

This requires very great care. The berries are put into a vessel that keeps turning round and round over the fire, so that they may not be in danger of getting burned.

While the berries are being roasted an oil comes from them, which gets, as it cools, as thick as butter.

There is a little story told about the coffee plant.

A learned Frenchman gave three plants to the captain of a ship to take to the West Indies.

He wanted the coffee plant to grow there as it did in Arabia.

The captain took great care of the three plants. But on the voyage all

THE CAPTAIN GIVING AWAY HIS ALLOWANCE OF WATER.

the fresh water on board was used up. Scarcely enough remained, to allow each man a draught of water a-day.

The poor coffee plants could not live without being watered. They drooped, and two of them died.

The captain was very anxious to save the last. He went without water himself, and gave the small quantity allowed him to the plant.

So the coffee plant was saved.

And, thanks to it, the people in the West Indies were able to grow coffee.

HOW DO THE ARABS DRESS?

How do the Arabs dress?

In summer, the men wear a cotton shirt. If a man is rich enough, he will put a long gown over his shirt. This gown will be made of cotton, or of silk, if he can afford it; but most of the Arabs wear a woollen mantle over their shirts.

These mantles are of all kinds and all colours. The grandest of them are woven with gold, and cost a great deal of money.

The Arab is very fond of shoes, though he seldom wears them. He likes them to be of some bright colour. A pair of yellow boots would delight him.

What does he wear on his head?

A square handkerchief. He folds it about his head, and makes a turban of it. One corner he lets fall backwards, and the two other corners hang down in front of his shoulders.

When the sun is hot, he can pull these corners over his face, and make a veil of them.

If he does not want to be seen, he can hide himself behind his handkerchief.

The handkerchief is a gay colour, such as yellow, or yellow mixed with green. Over it, the Arab ties a cord of camel's hair round his head.

HOW DO THE ARABS DRESS?

Some of the rich chiefs wear handsome striped shawls on their heads. They are very careful to protect their heads from the sun.

In winter, the Arab puts on some warmer clothes. He has a pelisse

ARABS OF SAHARA.

made of sheepskins sewed together. He can bear heat and cold in a very wonderful manner.

In the winter, when it is very cold, he will sleep in an open tent, with his feet bare, and without a fire.

In the summer, he will wrap his mantle round him, and lie down on the burning sand, in the full blaze of the sun, and go to sleep.

So strong and hardy are the children of the desert!

How do the women dress?

They wear a dark cotton gown, made very full. They have a handkerchief round their heads.

They are very fond of trinkets, and have silver rings in their ears and noses.

They prick their lips and dye them blue, by way of making themselves look handsome.

They wear veils over their faces, and glass beads round their wrists.

They have no shoes, but go about barefoot.

THE ARAB'S LANCE.

When an Arab pitches his tent, the first thing he does is to drive his lance into the ground outside.

The lance is the most important weapon the Arab has. When he is galloping in the desert, he will often brandish his lance.

His lance is made of wood, and has a sharp-pointed head of iron or steel. It will sometimes have a tuft of ostrich feathers near the top.

When an Arab is going to throw his lance, he balances it for a little time over his head; then he thrusts it forward. If the enemy is coming behind him, he will throw his lance backwards in a very dexterous manner. He will often kill his enemy's horse with one of these back-thrusts. There is nothing an Arab cannot do with his lance.

Has he any other weapons?

Yes; he has a sword which he carries everywhere with him. He bought it of some travelling pedlar, and very likely gave a great deal more for it than it was worth.

He does not go to his neighbour's tent, to drink a cup of coffee, without taking his sword.

He has a curved knife that he carries in his girdle.

These are his three weapons: his lance, his sword, and his knife.

THE ARAB'S LANCE.

The Arab knows the use of firearms, and can shoot with a gun. He lies down on the ground to shoot, and very seldom misses his aim.

He also uses a sling, and can throw a stone with great skill.

ARABS ROBBING A PALM GARDEN.

The shepherds often use a sling and a stone, to defend their flocks from the wild beasts.

Does not this remind you of King David, when he was a shepherd boy, and slew the giant with a sling and a stone?

The Bedouin Arabs may well be called the children of the sword.

It may be said of the Arab, as of his great ancestor Ishmael, "His hand is against every man, and every man's hand against him."

The people who go across the desert are always in dread of him. Unless they put themselves under the care of some powerful Arab chief, they are almost sure to get robbed.

WORKMEN IN THE DESERT.

A BEDOUIN ARAB is too proud to shoe his own horse or mend his saddle.

He must have a blacksmith, and a saddler, to do it for him. These workmen are not Arabs. They come from the villages near the desert, and spend the summer in the tents of the Arabs.

When the summer is over, they go back to their homes.

But the Arab thinks the workman far beneath himself in rank. He lets him shoe his horses, but he would not allow him to marry his daughter on any account.

If the workman wants a wife, he must marry one of the Arab's slaves, or else a woman of his own tribe.

There are a few useful arts which the Bedouin is not too proud to practise.

He can tan, and weave, and dye. No skin is ever dyed but that of the camel.

Shall I tell you how it is done?

The skin is covered with salt, and left for two or three days. Then it is steeped in a liquid paste made of barley meal and water.

Then it is washed in clean water, and all the hair got off.

Next, the Arab takes a great many pomegranates, pounds them and mixes them with the water. He lets the skin remain in the mixture several days. When it comes out it is yellow.

Water-bags are made of this dyed skin.

Goat's hair is used for the covering of the tents, and for many other purposes. The tent covers are worked by the women, in a rude kind of loom. The mother and her daughters will sit working in the tent.

Among the shepherds, the men will often employ themselves in weaving.

THE GREAT BIRD OF THE DESERT.

An Arab is a rich man when he has plenty of horses and camels.

His camel is called a dromedary. It has one hump, and is very swift indeed. When an Arab rides away on his camel, it is not easy to catch

THE OSTRICH.

him. The Arab horse is one of the swiftest horses in the world. The Arab looks upon it as his friend.

When it was a little foal it played about in the tent, and was like one

THE GREAT BIRD OF THE DESERT.

of the family. The children were very fond of it, and it was quite gentle, and never hurt them.

The Arab hunts the ostrich on horseback.

The ostrich is the great bird of the desert. Its long legs can get over the ground very quickly indeed. Its wings cannot raise it into the air, but they can help it along like the sail of a boat. The Arab wants its beautiful feathers to sell; and he wants its flesh to eat; and he likes to take its great eggs. He dare not touch them with his fingers. If he did, the mother-bird would find it out, and she would not lay any more eggs in that place. And she would be so angry, as to trample to pieces all the eggs he had left. He is obliged to be very cunning, and he pushes the eggs out of the nest with a long stick.

He can sell the eggs for a shilling a-piece.

It is very hard work to hunt the ostrich. The Arab horse is very strong as well as swift. But it has to go

HUNTING THE OSTRICH WITH A FALCON.

on running, often two or three days; and then it would never catch the great bird, if it were not for one thing.

The ostrich gets tired, and loses ground, because it keeps running from

THE GREAT BIRD OF THE DESERT.

one side to the other; so that in time the Arab and his horse gain upon it, and at last come up with it.

The easiest way of hunting the ostrich is to surround the flock.

A great many Arabs go out together, and ride to the place where they see the flock feeding.

Then they make a circle round it, and keep coming closer and closer.

At length they get so near that the birds are frightened, and begin to run against each other, and to dash madly about.

Then, the Arabs kill them with blows from a stick.

In some places, the hunter uses a falcon, or hawk, as you see in the picture.

What is the religion of the Arabs?

They worship the false prophet Mohammed.

CPSIA information can be obtained
at www.ICGtesting.com
Printed in the USA
BVHW091800170920
588700BV00032B/589